LET HER DIE

KILLING THE VERSION OF YOU THAT KEEPS YOU SMALL

MELISSA DEAN

MAGICSEEKER HOUSE

First Edition
Hardcover ISBN: 979-8-9994123-1-7
Paperback ISBN: 979-8-9994123-0-0
Cover design and illustrations created by Melissa Dean using AI-assisted tools (ChatGPT/DALL·E)
Interior layout by Melissa Dean
This work contains content developed with the assistance of artificial intelligence tools for editing. All final creative decisions, both written and visual, were made by the author.
Published by MagicSeeker House
Las Cruces, New Mexico

For more information, visit www.LetHerDie.com
For permissions or inquiries letherdiebook@gmail.com
Printed in the United States of America

Journey Markers

Disclaimer

This book is not intended as a substitute for professional medical, psychological, or mental health advice, diagnosis, or treatment. The content reflects the author's personal experiences and perspectives and is offered for educational and inspirational purposes only.

Always seek the advice of your physician, therapist, or other qualified health provider with any questions you may have regarding a mental health or medical condition. Never disregard professional advice or delay in seeking it because of something you've read in this book.

Healing is not linear, and there is no one-size-fits-all path. Trust yourself, take what resonates, and leave the rest.

I believe in showing up before you feel ready.

I believe in the beauty of the messy middle...the part of life no one posts about.

I believe in doing it scared, in feeling it all, and in not needing to make it look graceful.

I believe you don't have to be the loudest in the room to make an impact.

I believe that healing isn't linear, growth isn't always visible, and rest *is* productive.

I believe you don't need to be fixed...you just need to be seen.

I believe you are allowed to outgrow the version of yourself that kept you safe...and let her go when it's time.

I believe that softness isn't weakness and success isn't a performance.

I believe in saying the thing, feeling the thing, and *being* the thing, even when it's inconvenient.

I believe in starting over as many times as it takes.

And I believe that when you stop hiding, you don't become someone new...you bury who you're not, and rise up to become who you've always been.

To Koko
Thank you for being my mirror, my calm, and my constant. This book carries your voice just as much as mine. We both know this wouldn't exist without you.

To Mason, Mia, and Micah
May you always trust your knowing, speak your truth, and never shrink to fit someone else's version of enough.

To Crystal
For walking me through the threshold of a new way of thinking. For showing me tools that changed my life and for always holding space.

This wouldn't have been possible without you all.

I love you.

Read this if you've ever felt like too much, not enough, or both in the same breath.

This is a book about the death of the version of you that made everyone else comfortable and the quiet rebirth of the one who no longer needs to be understood. It's about awareness and unraveling. You know, that soft, slow kind of unraveling... where it doesn't announce itself but still changes everything. It's where we learn that self-abandonment looks a lot like politeness. It's the dreams we've shelved because wanting more felt selfish, dramatic, or too loud. It's how we hide and shrink ourselves down until we realize we've been slowly disappearing.

I didn't write this from the mountaintop. Hah, *not at all*. I wrote it from the messy middle where I felt like the walls were closing in on me. The *"what if it falls apart* days" and the *"why does this still hurt"* nights. I wrote it from the grey days and the grief. This is the kind of growth that doesn't come with applause.

I've spent years holding space for other people's healing...cheering them on and loving them through their growth. But when it came to my own? I stayed quiet. I shapeshifted or shrank until there wasn't a whole lot left of me. I didn't realize it, but I softened the edges of myself that were never meant to be dull. And I don't know when it happened exactly, but one day I decided she had to go. I had to let her die...and not in a morbid way, but rather, a "I need this for myself" way.

Once you make that decision, the Universe (or God, or Entity/Source - whatever feels right for you) starts conspiring in your favor. And somewhere in my unfolding, I started taking notes, not to teach or perform, but just to remember what helped me breathe again. What grounded me and reminded me that I'm allowed to take up space. The mindset shifts that let me rest. The moments I didn't think I'd get through or being terrified of what waited on the other side.

This book is a collection of those notes. It's for anyone who's ever asked, "*Why can't I just get out of my own way?*" Anyone who's outgrown their hiding places or dimmed their light to make others more comfortable. Anyone who's ever felt like the outsider in their own story.

You don't need to be healed to begin. You don't need to have it all figured out. You definitely don't need a new identity or a plan to "fix" yourself.

You just need to tell the truth...and let the version of you that was never free, finally rest.

In the chapters ahead, we'll be talking about ego, overthinking, money wounds, self-talk, grief, body image, joy, identity, and what it really means to live a life that's yours. Not perfect or performative. Just real.

Let's walk through it together.

INTRODUCTION

I'm the type who plays every scenario in my head before it happens, like some twisted rehearsal for disappointment. I can feel everything in a room and still wonder if I'm making it up. I overanalyze compliments, never allowing myself to accept them at face value; I'm always waiting for the "catch". I replay conversations in the shower. I imagine worst-case outcomes like I'm directing a short film no one asked for.

I'm not just sensitive, I'm highly tuned. My brain wants to know the rules, the risks, the temperature, the tone and it's exhausting sometimes.

But it's also why I see people the way I do. Why I notice the cracks they try to hide. Why I can hold space for others the way I needed someone to hold it for me.

I'm a mom of three, a wife, and a boudoir photographer who watches quietly, feels deeply, and sometimes overthinks it all. I've been known to deliver tough love wrapped in kind words to help others see their potential. It's been coined as a motivational beatdown. I'm a bit on the woo-woo side and I believe in the Universe's energy. Weed (I know, I know...the industry prefers cannabis, but let's be real - weed feels more honest to me) is a daily part of my life. It's not my identity, but it is part of my healing. I do believe weed is medicine whether you use it recreationally or not.

This book is primarily geared toward women based on my personal experiences, but I believe the lessons here can benefit anyone on a healing journey.

I wanted to be seen and invisible at the same time. I wanted to be honest but still liked. I wanted to create something raw but worried people wouldn't get it. Looking back, I realize I wasn't just scared of failing, I was scared of trying. Because trying meant admitting I cared. And if I cared, I could lose something.

Have you ever said no to something that lit you up, just because it felt too big for who you thought you were allowed to be?

Let's go back a bit.

It was early 2023. The initial spark for writing this book came unexpectedly (as moments of clarity often do). It was a typical evening in the garage with my husband, Koko, where our nightly chats often veer into the philosophical. We playfully call these our "universal portal" sessions, where we tap into deeper truths that evade us during the rush of the day. Our daughter, Mia, joined us that evening, her mind preoccupied with the upcoming Regional ID Camp for soccer. Seeking guidance from the Universe, she asked to pull an oracle card. Flipping through the deck, she was called to one that caught her eye. She handed it to me and I flipped it over, "Destruction." It sparked a 30-minute conversation about breaking through limiting beliefs and showing up as you are. Satisfied with her message, she headed to bed. We continued with the conversation which eventually led Koko to utter the phrase "hiding from success." A rush pulsed through my body and I knew I had to start taking notes.

My journey to this point has been marked by moments of insecurity and self-doubt. During my teenage years, I struggled deeply with feelings of inadequacy, regularly trying to figure out where I belonged, and often tying my self-worth to the success of my friendships and relationships. In my late teens I would be diagnosed with depression and anxiety. I wrestled with the effects of antidepressants that seemed to numb rather than heal. I was a shell of myself. It wasn't until I discovered weed, initially used recreationally, that I started to realize it wasn't just about enjoyment, it *was* medicine. However, it would be years before I would start on my journey toward healing and find my way to therapy.

As an artist and observer, storytelling through photography became my medium of choice. For over a decade, I would explore different niches of photography, from high school seniors to weddings, sports photography, and everything in between. After 2020 we found ourselves needing to pivot and began photographing in the cannabis realm where eventually Koko and I would get picked up to run the marketing of a local cannabis dispensary. In the midst of that era, I had an experience with a dear friend, Chelsie, that sparked my soul in ways that I wasn't anticipating. The session was a raw, authentic exploration that resonated deeply with both of us, sparking a new direction in my professional and personal life. She wanted to do a shoot that celebrated the era in her life that she was currently in. A shoot deeply personal and raw. I was intrigued, and even though I had never done anything quite like *this* before, I agreed, and we went for it. We were vulnerable. She wanted to fully embrace her insecurities. Her message to me spoke so deeply. "I'd like to do a realistic boudoir shoot. It's hard for me, but I feel like I want to emphasize my imperfections. I have stretch marks all over my stomach and thighs that have bothered me in the past but don't seem to anymore." Internally I was already invested. She is such a beautiful soul, and I was thrilled that we were going to reach a new level together. I was excited, yes, but I was also resisting. Part of me felt like a fraud. Like who was I to hold space for someone else's vulnerability when I was still hiding behind my own?

I almost canceled. Told myself it wasn't the right time, that I needed to be "more healed" before diving into work like this. But something kept pulling at me. Then, she tried to cancel and from that point, I knew we were both being called to something more. I recognized the fear she and I both were experiencing. That doubting voice that was trying to stop us both from doing something *new* and *scary*. I literally told her, "Buckle up, because we're going on this ride".

That session didn't just change her, it cracked something open in *me*. Something I wasn't ready for, but desperately needed.

The session happened and honestly, I was not prepared for what it was going to do to me. The energy was palpable. It was radiating through us both. During the week, I couldn't shake this feeling that I was being called to explore this a little deeper. I couldn't stop thinking about how the session made me feel and how it made her feel, and she hadn't even **seen** the photos! I wanted more. I had to dive in. So, I started something from (what felt like) square one again. I created Melissa Dean Boudoir. A new venture *way* out of my comfort zone, but

I couldn't ignore the call.

The truth is I struggle with doing things on my own. I'm a perfectionist. I don't like being seen. I hide behind my camera. In the spirit of being vulnerable, I decided it was time for me to stop hiding and put myself out there. Using my own name felt terrifying. I wasn't just building a business, I was attaching my entire identity to something public. Permanent. Exposed. In the past, I could hide behind a clever business name. Something I made up. Something safe. If it failed or flopped or got misunderstood... at least it wasn't *me*. But this time? I had to lean in. I used *my* name. No more hiding behind the brand. No more putting a buffer between who I am and what I do.

I kept thinking:
What if they don't get it?
What if they think it's too much?
What if they think I'm too much?

But another voice, quieter but steadier, whispered back:
And what if they love it?
What if this is exactly what someone else needs to see?

That's when I decided: I'd rather be fully seen and misunderstood than invisible and safe.

So, I finally started the new branch. It was time to be seen. Fully, honestly, and imperfectly. I created a business that *is* me. A space that is safe to talk about real shit. A space where we can create beautiful art together. A space where you can be unapologetically you and I can be unapologetically me. I want to empower each other. I want women to do the scary thing. I want us to forget about what society says is beautiful. I want us to stop hiding behind roles or brands or masks that aren't ours. I want to help you overcome the fear and be honest about who we are. Because when I embraced vulnerability, I realized the power of stepping out from behind that shield. This book is part of that same commitment. A journey from behind-the-scenes to fully *in* the scene. A story of stepping into the light, even when it shakes you. And maybe... an invitation for you to do the same.

A Quick Note

Writing this book has made me reflect on the real power of boudoir, not just for others, but for me. It's where the healing started. It's not just about capturing moments; it's about empowering individuals to see themselves with compassion and courage. I encourage everyone, men and women alike, to consider an individual boudoir shoot; and not just for the photographs, but for the profound shift it can ignite within. If that's out of your comfort zone, good! I know it's vulnerable. I get it. I've been there too. We are our own worst critic. But I'm so glad you're reading this, because hopefully this is the first step toward an amazing journey that will forever change the way you see yourself. Boudoir sessions are an experience. The experience ultimately depends on the photographer, so read those reviews and make sure you vibe with them! You are going to emerge from this feeling stronger than you could possibly know. I know it's scary. I'm sure you're already thinking "maybe when I lose 10 pounds" or "I'm not pretty enough." BUT it takes doing the uncomfortable things to grow. It takes facing your fears. Leading up to your session you may struggle with: doubt, insecurity, panic, overthinking, unworthiness, but you'll emerge feeling: energy, release, love, empowered, and peace. I see so many women lose their power. They fall into a cycle of being just a soccer mom, or just a wife, or just a career woman. We are not *just* any one thing. It's time to take back your power. Your femininity. Your love for yourself. Let's share a journey together. I'll be here cheering you on. Dancing with you. Embracing all the flaws that make us the women we are. You are your own vibe. Let's dive in.

We're going to start by diving into what we're really healing from. Let's be real, this book isn't just about success. It's about everything that gets in the way of it. The buried stuff. The things we don't say out loud. The stuff we've normalized because we're highly functioning and self-aware and *still* stuck. This is about letting *her* die...the version of you who learned to shrink in the name of survival.

These are the things we're healing from:

Thinking errors – The mental loops that make us feel like we have to be perfect, prepared, or "ready" before we try.

Self-doubt – That constant inner hum that says *maybe I'm not enough...* even when we're doing all the things.

Self-image issues – Not just our bodies, but the way we've learned to *see* ourselves through warped lenses.

Guilt for wanting more – Especially when life doesn't look "bad."

Fear of visibility – Because being seen means being judged. Or misunderstood. Or rejected.

A distorted relationship with failure – Where mistakes feel like proof that we should've never tried.

And here's another thing I've had to unlearn. I used to worry that I wasn't saying anything new. That maybe I was just echoing what had already been said, sometimes by people louder, shinier, or more "qualified" than me. But I've come to understand something that changed everything, the Universe repeats itself on purpose. The truth doesn't need a single messenger, it needs many. Messages are seeded across souls, whispered into different lives, and carried through different experiences so they can reach the people they're meant to reach. We all hang in different circles. We touch different hearts. And even if we're sharing similar truths, they're still being delivered in a voice only we can offer.

So if you've ever felt like your truth is too familiar, or your story's already been told, this is your permission to say it anyway. It's not about being the first. It's about being *real*. Your voice is a delivery method and someone out there is waiting to hear it *from you*.

I'm not claiming to have mastered all of this. I still get tangled up. But what I *have* found are tools that help me untangle faster. That help me sit with the spiral without letting it suck me in. That help me take down the ego one whisper at a time.

That's what these chapters are. A battle with the old stories. A step-by-step way of saying: *we don't do that anymore.* That session I talked about earlier cracked something open in me- and not just creatively. It stirred something deeper. Something uncomfortable. It's like my soul stood up... and my ego panicked.

Because here's the truth:

The moment I decided to stop hiding...from myself, from others, from the work I knew I was meant to do, that's when she really showed up.

My ego.

She didn't storm in with fireworks. She crept in like smoke.

And just when I was starting to step into alignment...she dropped the line she always does, "Let's not get carried away." So, before I could go any further and before I could build anything with integrity or move forward with courage, I had to face her. I had to meet the version of me that wanted to stay safe...and learn how to walk forward anyway.

IDENTIFYING YOUR EGO

Have you ever had that little voice inside your head that tells you you're not good enough, not ready, or not worthy? Yeah, me too. I've learned to call her my Ego. Not ego, like "they are so full of themselves" ego. Ego, as in, that internal, doubting voice that just won't quit.

My ego is snarky. A little cold. Always standing there with her arms crossed, looking down on me like she's waiting for me to screw up. She doesn't scream, she condescends. And somehow, that makes it worse.
"Who are you kidding?"
"You're not good enough."
"This is a waste of time, and you know it."

That's her voice. She's steady. Cynical. Familiar. For a long time, I thought she was the rational part of me, you know, the *informed* voice, the one helping me make *responsible* decisions. But the truth is, she was just fear in a nicer outfit. She disguised herself as logic and dressed up like protection and she was holding me back. Over and over again.

When I first started photographing women, vulnerably, in this space, I noticed something interesting. It didn't matter if they were CEOs or stay-at-home moms, classically beautiful or self-described "awkward", outgoing or quiet...they all said the same kinds of things about themselves. "I'm not photogenic." "Sorry, I'm so awkward." "Can you just Photoshop that?" "I hate my arms."

Almost every single woman could stand in front of my camera and *easily* fire off everything she <u>hated</u> about herself. It became so predictable I could've written the script for them. And at first, I thought, maybe this is just nerves, maybe it's temporary. But the more I listened and the more I actually heard what they were saying, the more I realized this wasn't just about photos.

This was deeply ingrained. A pattern. A script we were taught. Somewhere along the way, we all got handed the same damn rulebook:
• Downplay your beauty.
• Deflect compliments.
• Stay humble...but like, the fake kind.
• Don't be too much.
• Don't love yourself too loudly.

What started as my work behind the camera turned into something much bigger. As I handed women their photos and watched them see themselves through a new lens, I realized:

Oh. *I've healed from some of this.*

And it wasn't random. It was through tools. Through work. Through reclaiming parts of myself I had silenced so long ago. Every single client was giving me insight...into their self-talk, their beliefs, their confidence. And I started to dig deeper. Through questionnaires, conversations, and what felt like hundreds of micro-therapy sessions disguised as photo shoots, I kept seeing the same core wound:

Negative self-talk wasn't a personality trait, it was taught. We learned this stuff.

False modesty wasn't humility; it was a muzzle. All these habits were carefully conditioned to keep us small and palatable. Acceptable. And once I started seeing it that way, I realized... it had a voice. A specific one. One I'd known for a long time. I just didn't know it had a name.

Ego.

The ego's job is to keep us safe. But the way she does it? It's outdated. She thrives on what's familiar, even if it's not working anymore. She doesn't want you to grow. She wants you to stay small, predictable, unexposed. And for a while, I didn't even notice she was there. It wasn't some lightning-bolt realization, it was much slower than that.

I think I saw a reel or quote that hinted at the idea that Ego isn't what we think it is. That it's not just arrogance, it's the narrator of our inner dialogue. The gatekeeper of safety. That shifted something in me. I started recognizing her voice. Naming it. And eventually, becoming disillusioned by it. I started noticing that fear was dictating most of my thoughts. Ego had been running the show under the guise of caution, logic, even self-care. And I'd been listening without question.

The more I started breaking out of comfort zones, whether it was launching something, sharing something vulnerable, or showing up fully in my work, the louder she got. And that's when I realized something: Her volume goes up when I'm on the edge of something bigger. Not because I'm doing the wrong thing, but because I'm doing the brave thing. And she hates brave. Ego plays on our insecurities. She knows our wounds. She's not some stranger...she's lived in us for so long that she knows exactly where to press.

She doesn't need new material; she just replays the same old doubts, wrapped in fresh packaging. She remembers the things people said when we were too young to question them. The comments that landed like truth and stuck like glue. That's her script. She's a shapeshifter, and here's the part that catches so many of us off guard: she doesn't always show up as a loud inner critic. Sometimes she's soft and familiar. Even sneaky.

She doesn't necessarily barge in with red flags and blaring alarms. Instead, she slips in like a weighted blanket, soft and comfortable. She speaks in the tone of your childhood comfort, using the same language that once made you feel safe. It's not always "You're not good enough." Sometimes it's: "Let's not do this today. You've had a long week." Or "You can't handle that right now." It may even be that comforting hand softly tapping on your shoulder: "Better to wait until it's perfect."

She disguises herself as reason. She cloaks herself in concern. She doesn't need to tear you down. She just needs you to stay still. Sometimes she wears the face of your mother, your coach, your ex, the people who once wanted to protect you, or the ones who broke you. She speaks in voices that feel like truth because you've heard them so many times, they've become background noise. She's the one who hands you a cozy excuse when you're about to do something brave. She pats your head when you're trying to break old patterns.

She's the one saying, "Take the day off," but only on the days you're about to push forward. And that's why she's dangerous—because her goal isn't to destroy you. It's to preserve you. But not the version of you that's growing. The version of you that's just surviving.

Let's talk about when she shows up as self-doubt. Not the loud or dramatic kind, just... there. That little nudge. A breath that pulls you back a step.

"Are you sure you're the right person for this?"
"What if you fail again?"
"What makes you think you're ready?"

It's not the volume that gets you, it's the timing. She knows *exactly* when to lean in. Right after a big idea. Right before you hit "send." Right when you're about to say yes to something that scares you just enough to matter. She plants the seed that maybe you're not the one. That maybe this dream was meant for someone more experienced, more charismatic, more qualified.

She doesn't scream "No." She just gently asks, "But why you?" And because it sounds like a reasonable question, you entertain it. So... you go quiet. You stall. You start looking outward for proof that you belong, instead of inward for the truth that you already do. And that's how she wins. Not by stopping you, but by getting you to stop yourself. She's not interested in drama. She prefers the slow slide back into smallness. The kind that looks like perfectionism. Or comparison. The kind that has you doubting your timing, your tone, or your worth. Sometimes she shows up as procrastination. Not because you're lazy, but because she's stalling. She knows that putting things off delays the risk. If you don't start, you can't fail. If you stay in planning mode, you don't have to deal with the mess of doing. Because doing *is* messy. Doing means feedback. Visibility. Vulnerability. And she hates all of that. So instead, she'll convince you to keep refining the idea. To keep organizing the to-do list. To keep lighting candles and making the perfect playlist before you start.

She'll have you cleaning the junk drawer instead of sending the email (or writing the damn book). Scrolling instead of creating. Learning instead of applying. She'll whisper things like: "You're just not ready yet." "Let's wait until things calm down." "Once you have more time... more energy... more clarity... then you'll start."

And while it might feel like you're being thoughtful or intentional, what you're really doing is avoiding the discomfort of momentum. Because once you start moving, you can't un-know that you're capable. And when you're capable, you have to face the fear of what's next. That next step. The next stretch. The next version of you. And she's not ready to let go of the current one. Not yet. Sometimes she even disguises herself as 'self-care.' She'll tell you:

"You're too tired to do this today."
"You deserve a break... don't push yourself."
"This is just your body protecting you."

And while those statements can be true, when Ego's in charge, they're not coming from a place of nourishment. They're coming from avoidance. That's why I call it "retreat dressed as rest." She's clever like that. She knows how to blend in with your inner dialogue, use your language, and speak in your tone. She can even use your healing tools against you. That's why awareness is everything. You don't have to banish her. You just have to recognize when she's shape-shifting and call her out.

***

Chapter 1: Part two

Want to know the cruelest part? Sometimes she sounds like concern. Like she's protecting you from embarrassment or regret. But what she's really protecting is your current identity. She doesn't want you to risk stepping into something bigger, because that would mean shedding the version of you she knows how to manage. So when you hear her whispering those familiar doubts, don't argue, observe. Become aware. Answer her gently: "I hear you. But I'm doing it anyway."

Not because you're fearless. Because you've finally decided to believe in the version of you that she's afraid of. She convinced me I wasn't strong enough, brave enough, talented enough. When I started to stretch, she'd pull out the file cabinet of failures and say, "Remember that one time you tried and it didn't work?" And the worst part is, I believed her. Without hesitation. I let her talk me out of things I was built for. Sometimes, she even pretended to have my best interest in mind. She told me to stay in a relationship I had no business being in. "This is as good as it gets," she'd say. "Nobody else is going to love you." So I shrank. I stayed. I convinced myself that being alone was scarier than being unseen. That's not safety. That's self-abandonment dressed up as practicality.

And she's especially loud when I'm tired or alone. She becomes a relentless loop of "should haves" and "why didn't yous." But when I'm winning?

Oh, then she becomes smug.

"I knew you could do it all along," she'll say...conveniently forgetting the fight I had to have with her to even try.

That's the thing about Ego. She always wants the last word, no matter which side she's on. But here's the trick that changed everything for me: I stopped trying to get rid of her. And I started talking to her. When she gets loud now, I say things like: "I know this is fear. I know you're trying to keep me safe." I literally say it out loud. Sometimes I do it in the garage with Koko. I lay it all out, say the things I'm afraid of, and he helps me sort through what's true and what's Ego. She hates that, by the way. Because when you name her, you take her power. You stop mistaking her voice for truth.

And here's the thing, your ego isn't the villain. She's just scared.

She's the part of you that learned to expect disappointment and prepares for the worst, so you won't be caught off guard. She's the echo of generational fear, especially if, like me, you were raised in a "worst-case-scenario" household. She means well, really, she does. Her whole job is to keep you safe. But she is so tired, whether she admits it or not. She's afraid that if we succeed, it means she wasted all those years protecting us for nothing. She's afraid she'll lose her place at the table. That we'll look back and see the opportunities she made us miss. So she clings. But you don't have to obey her. Not anymore. You can thank her for her service...and then kindly ask her to sit down.

You can say, "Sorry Ego, I appreciate your concern, but you don't run the show anymore." You can remind her (and yourself) of everything you've already survived. Every step you've already taken. Every fear you've walked through and come out the other side. Because you've already done hard things. You've gone after things she swore you couldn't. You've shown up anyway. And the more you do that, the more her voice starts to fade.

Don't get me wrong...she'll still show up, especially when you're growing. But she won't get the final word. That belongs to you now.

***

I want you to close your eyes and imagine two rooms.

Room One is dim, quiet, and way too familiar. You know every inch of it. It's a shelter. The dreams you shoved in drawers and the post-it notes of "maybe someday" taped to the walls.

It's safe, sure, but it's suffocating. It's where you've kept yourself small enough to be unbothered. You don't even have to lock the door, because your ego's already standing there (like she does), arms crossed, dead serious, guarding you like you're some fragile thing. She's tired, honestly. But she won't sit down. She's been doing this job so long, she doesn't know how to stop.

7

You might still love her. Hell, you might even thank her. But you know damn well you can't live by her anymore.

Now...

Room Two? It's bright. Not just like "sunlight" bright. But the kind of light that feels like truth. Like calling. Like *finally*. It's warm. Open. It kind of hits your nervous system like, "Wait... I'm allowed to feel this good?" There are windows everywhere. That dopamine decor that lights you up just hits. You can breathe in here. And right in the middle? A mirror. But not the kind that shows you the version of yourself you've been tolerating. This mirror shows you the version that's been waiting. The one with the fire behind her eyes. The one you almost became a hundred times but kept talking yourself out of. She looks like you, of course...but more you. She's not just a possibility. She's a memory, pulling you forward. And she's been waiting for you to show up.

Reflection

This isn't about fixing what's wrong with you. This is about recognizing what's been running the show...and gently taking the mic back. You're not broken. There's nothing wrong with you. You've just been surviving. And now... you're waking up.

Let's get real:

• What does your ego actually sound like? What are her go-to lines? Her favorite excuses?
• What fear is she trying to protect you from? (And does it even belong to you?)
• Where do you feel her in your body? What shifts when she's calling the shots?
• What would it look like to thank her... and do the thing anyway?

• What's one old tape she keeps replaying... and what new truth are you ready to replace it with?
• What's something brave she tried to stop, but you did it anyway? How did that feel?

And if nothing else, ask yourself this: Are you living in the room you've outgrown... or the one you've been waiting for? You're not here to barely survive. You're here to remember who you've always been.

Once I started recognizing Ego's voice (and realizing how long I'd let her run the show)I noticed something else, too. She wasn't just whispering doubts into new experiences. She was also the one pressing play on the old tapes. The worn-out narratives. The beliefs I didn't even know I was still carrying. The phrases that slipped into my mind without question and stayed there long enough to feel like mine...Like the way I picked myself apart before anyone else could. Or the way I rehearsed rejection so it wouldn't hurt as bad when it came. Ego didn't just live in my fear. She lived in my habits. In the cruel rituals of how I talked to myself. And most days, I didn't even notice.

That's the thing about old programming: it runs quietly in the background... until someone flips the breaker. You don't realize how loud the voice has been until you hear someone speak to you with kindness and it doesn't sound familiar.

That's what happened the day my daughter walked into the bathroom where I was getting ready and interrupted a decades-old mental loop. What she said wasn't just love...it was disruption. And what I said next became one of the most powerful mindset shifts I've ever used.

We don't do that anymore.

CHAPTER TWO

WE DON'T DO THAT ANYMORE

C hange is hard. Not because we're weak, but because we're wired to repeat. We're creatures of habit, even when the habit is hating ourselves. It's like some worn-out song you've heard a thousand times in the background of your life. You get so used to it, you don't even realize you've been dancing to a rhythm that doesn't fit anymore. But just because it's familiar doesn't mean it's right for you. And honestly? A lot of what we're still doing is just survival.

I can't remember when this first clicked in for me, but I do remember I was standing in front of the mirror, internally tearing myself apart. "Look at those wrinkles on your forehead...ugh and your stomach...you've really let yourself go... are those grey hairs now too?!" It wasn't new. It was *background noise*. The kind I didn't question anymore.

Then my daughter casually walked in unaware of my ritual of self-hate and came and hugged me, "You're so beautiful, Mama," and squeezed me even tighter as if she could hear my internal monologue.

I wanted to believe her. But the voice in my head was louder. And the thing is, it wasn't even my own voice, not originally. It was layered. Pieces of magazines, little side comments, middle school insults, backhanded compliments from family members. I'd absorbed them all so deeply that by the time I was an adult, they all sounded like truth.

And that's when it hit me. She wasn't *just* hugging me. She was interrupting the cycle. Standing there like a mirror, reflecting the love I forgot how to give myself. Where did I learn to be so cruel to my body? And more importantly, what would she learn from me if I didn't stop? What would *all* of my kids learn from me if I didn't stop? Because it's not just about raising daughters who know their worth, it's about raising sons who don't internalize toxic ideas about worth, control, masculinity, or appearance either. I want them to see what self-respect looks like. What boundaries look like. What softness looks like without shame. I want them to grow up knowing that emotions aren't weaknesses, that self-worth isn't measured by productivity or how much you achieve. I want them to know that being kind to yourself doesn't make you fragile, it makes you free. Compassion, toward others and themselves, is powerful as hell.

Then it occurred to me, how often does this happen? How often do I allow this part of my ego to creep in. She's pretty mean. What kind of example am I setting? Where did this even start?

That moment with my daughter was a wake-up call. I started paying attention to my inner dialogue and realized how often it was filled with criticism and negativity. This inner critic, this part of me that always had something negative to say, had become a constant companion. It was time to part ways.

The first step in breaking free from these habits was recognizing them. I had to become aware of the negative self-talk and the damaging beliefs that were running on autopilot in my mind. This wasn't easy, and it took a lot of conscious effort to catch myself in the act.

Enter, "We don't do that anymore."

"We don't do that anymore" is arguably one of my most important tools. I bring up this tool in almost every one of my sessions and that's why this is one of the first things we're going to talk about here, too. When I started incorporating this into my life, I slowly began to see the transformative change that was underway.

Here's how it works.

It starts with awareness, which we talked about earlier. This is the most crucial step. You have to hunt that negative voice down. You must be aware when she's creeping in. Then you have to stop her in her tracks. Let me be clear, this isn't some Pinterest quote or affirmation. This is *a line in the sand*. This phrase becomes a shift. A boundary and a tool. I started using it in the mirror, in the car, and in the studio. At first, it felt weird, but I swear it works.

Step 1: Identify the Negative Thoughts Pay attention to the thoughts running through your mind. Are they kind, supportive, and encouraging? Or are they critical, harsh, and filled with self-doubt? Write them down if you have to. This helps in making them tangible and easier to confront.

Step 2: Stop Her in Her Tracks Once you've identified the negative thoughts, the next step is to acknowledge them (and catch them early enough to interrupt them – but don't worry this will come with time). From there, we say "We don't do that anymore." I know it sounds crazy, saying "we," but you are talking to that personified ego, and telling her, "No, we DON'T do that anymore!" This process helps in breaking the cycle and power of the negative thought and puts you in charge of it.

Step 3: Replace with Positive Affirmations Now that you've challenged the negative thought, replace it with a positive affirmation. For example, if your inner critic says, "You're not good enough," interrupt her with, "No, we don't do that anymore. I am beautiful. I am worthy. I am enough." Yes, I'm sure you've heard those phrases grouped together before. I'm not saying I invented the wheel. But that's a good start if you're new to this. These positive affirmations serve as a powerful antidote to negativity.

One of my favorite ways to use this is when I am looking in the mirror. I inevitably still struggle with body image from time to time (remember healing isn't linear!) and I hear that inner voice criticizing me. I can almost guarantee that the voice you hear comes from somebody else. It's a belief that is so ingrained in you, that now it even sounds like you. Try to figure out whose voice it is. Where did you hear it first? What made you start believing it? Is it a collection of thoughts you've gathered over the years? Because for most of us, it is.

"Oh Hey Ego, yup I see you for what you are now!"

Remember, it's not just your voice! It could be your family's offhand comments, your aunt's diet talk, the kid in 7th grade who pointed something out you hadn't even noticed until then. It's the magazine covers at checkout stands and influencers in filtered lighting pretending it's effortless. It's decades of subtle programming that told us our bodies were projects, things to fix, things to shrink, and things to apologize for.

So when you hear that voice, when she starts picking you apart under fluorescent lighting or whispering bullshit while you're brushing your teeth, I want you to stop and ask: *Is this true? Or is this just familiar?* Because familiarity is not the same as truth. And just because it's been around a long time doesn't mean it belongs.

You get to question it now. You get to notice when Ego is shape-shifting into that mirror critic from Chapter One. You get to look her straight in the eye and say, "Hey. I know who you are. And we don't do that anymore." This is how you start reclaiming the mirror. One belief. One voice. One reflection at a time.

Now it's time to take your power back. Ask yourself:

- Why did that person say those things?

- Do you respect that person's opinions today?

- If so, do you think that is a good person to keep in your circle?

- If not, why are you letting their words and opinions hold weight over you?

- It's possible that she still sounds like your voice, and that's okay – but ask yourself, is this the pattern you want to keep allowing?

- Are these my thoughts, or is this coming from something else?

Like any new habit, this requires consistent practice. You might not see a change overnight, but with persistence, you'll start to notice a shift in your mindset. The more you practice, the easier it becomes to silence the inner critic and replace her voice with one of support and encouragement.

A Peek in the Studio

I had a client, let's call her Sara, who struggled with intense self-doubt. She constantly criticized herself and felt unworthy of love and success. She felt her voice shouldn't be heard. She allowed the perception of others to control her. We started incorporating "We don't do that anymore" into our session. She kept apologizing for everything. For her body. Her nerves. Her voice. For even existing in the space.

It was constant, "I hate my cellulite," "My stomach's gross," "I'm sorry I look like this" Or even when she wasn't saying it, but I could see her internal thoughts were wreaking havoc, I stopped her. Gently. But firmly. "Say it." I told her. She looked at me, confused. I nodded, "Say it with me: We don't do that anymore."

At first, she laughed. Rolled her eyes. Tried to brush it off.

But by the *fifteenth time*, it wasn't a joke anymore.

It became a mantra.

She started saying it on her own in the studio. Loud. Like she meant it. And something in her shifted. I saw it in her body. She *unclenched*. She softened. She started showing up like she belonged in her own skin again. I challenged her to do this for a month. Every. Single. Time she heard that negative voice creep in. Over the next few weeks, Sara began to notice a significant change in her mindset. She became more confident, started taking risks, and her self-esteem soared.

Weeks later, she messaged me:

"I say it almost every day now. It's changed everything. I don't let that voice run the show anymore. We don't do that anymore."

She was ecstatic. Here's the thing. You don't break these patterns overnight. You don't say the words once and become a whole new person.

But you do shift.

You start hearing yourself more clearly. You pause more often. You get better at catching the old programming before it spirals into self-sabotage. You start building new reflexes. And they will take you further than any perfectly crafted affirmation ever could.

And I told her what I'm telling you: It doesn't happen all at once. But it does happen. Changing ingrained habits and beliefs requires commitment. You have to be willing to put in the work and stay consistent. It's not about perfection; it's about progress. Progress happens with consistency. Celebrate the small victories along the way and be kind to yourself during setbacks.

Surround yourself with positivity. This means being mindful of the people you spend time with, the content you consume, and the environment you create for yourself. Supportive friends, uplifting books, and a positive workspace can make a huge difference in your journey towards change. Healing can be lonely. Especially as you shift out of old thinking patterns, you will notice that you no longer align with some of your core people. It's important to be aware of this. I'm not saying you have to completely cut them out of your life, but you do need to set some boundaries, or you will allow yourself to be anchored down.

As we continue this journey together, remember that breaking free from old habits and beliefs is a process. It takes time, effort, and patience. You have the power to change your story. You have the power to say, "We don't do that anymore," and create a new, positive way of thinking and being. This journey is about reclaiming your power, stepping out of hiding, and embracing your true potential. You've got this.

Healing isn't about becoming a shiny new version of yourself. It's about returning to the one that was always underneath the noise. The one who's been waiting for you to listen. The one who knows the truth. And the truth is: You don't need to stay in survival mode. You're allowed to walk out of that room.

Reflection:

Before you move on, pause for a second. What's one recurring thought or behavior in your life that no longer serves you? Say it out loud.

Now tell yourself: **"We don't do that anymore."**

You'll start to notice something the more you use this.

You'll catch more thoughts mid-sentence. You'll interrupt spirals you used to ride all the way to burn out. You'll start pausing before reacting. Here are some questions that might help.

- What version of self-talk do I want my kids (or future kids) to internalize from watching me? *What would I hope they say to themselves one day when they look in the mirror?*

- What messages did I receive growing up that I now recognize were harmful—even if they were unintentional? *What am I still carrying that it's time to release?*

- Whose voice is still lingering in my head—and does that person deserve to live rent-free in my mind anymore?

- What does being a cycle-breaker look like for me? *What beliefs, patterns, or behaviors stop with me?*

- If my child spoke to themselves the way I sometimes speak to myself... how would I respond?

- What's one belief I've repeated to myself that no longer feels true, but still shows up like it's mine?

- Where did I first learn to be critical of myself? Was it a person, a moment, or a pattern?

- What would it feel like to believe I am enough *without* conditions?

- What are three things I would never say to a friend, but often say to myself? (or if you heard a friend speaking to herself that way, how would you react?)

- When my inner critic shows up, what does she sound like? What does she want me to believe?

- How does my body respond when I speak kindly to it? How does it respond when I don't?

- What does "we don't do that anymore" mean to me right now? What thought, behavior, or pattern am I ready to interrupt?

- Is this thought true or is it just familiar?

You don't have to heal all at once. You just have to wake up a little more every time she tries to pull you back to sleep. And when she does? You know what to say.

We don't do that anymore.

But here's the thing: Some patterns run deeper than just insecurity. Some habits are rooted in exhaustion and overwhelm or in chronic overextension.

Sometimes it's not your inner critic talking, it's your nervous system waving a white flag. And in those moments, you need another tool. Something even simpler. Even faster. Because when the inner critic isn't the culprit, when it's just your soul begging for rest, there's one more tool I always reach for.

Just one question: **"Was that helpful?"**

CHAPTER THREE

WAS THAT HELPFUL?

Y ou ever catch yourself spiraling and think, "How the hell did I get here?" One minute you're just living your life, answering emails, making lunches, getting gas, and the next thing you know, your brain's whispering sweet nothings like: "You're a failure." "You're behind." "You should've done more." "Everyone's doing better than you."

Cool. Love that for us.

But here's what I've started doing. When that spiral creeps in (when the voice sounds responsible but feels like panic) I pause and ask one thing..."Is this helpful?"

Imagine your mind like a crowded room. Every thought is a voice. Some are shouting. Some are whispering. Some feel familiar, even comforting... others, not so much.

But over in the corner, there's a quieter voice. Calm. Neutral. Not judging...just curious. And it asks one simple question, "Is this helping?" That's the voice we're tuning into now. Change is a process. Are you seeing a theme here? The journey to personal growth involves questioning these habits and asking ourselves questions to pull us back into the present.

I remember a specific instance when I was feeling overwhelmed with the de-

mands of life. My business was booming, my kids needed my attention, and I felt like I was being pulled in a million different directions. I was juggling so many responsibilities that I barely had time to breathe. One evening, after a particularly exhausting day, I found myself in a cycle of negative thoughts:
"You're failing as a mom."
"You're not doing enough for your business."
"You're letting everyone down."

In the midst of that mental spiral, I paused and asked myself, "Is this helpful?" The answer was a resounding no. Those thoughts weren't helping me, honestly, they were only adding to my stress and anxiety. That simple question became a turning point. A new tool for the toolbox. It allowed me to step back and evaluate the impact of my thoughts and behaviors.

I used to hit that spiral hard anytime money was tight. It was automatic, like the moment the bank account dipped, so did my sense of worth. I'd start spinning. "You're failing the kids." "You're not pulling your weight." "You should be doing more." And every time, that voice sounded so responsible, like it was helping me hustle or stay focused, but it wasn't. It was just shame and it was pulling me away from what actually matters to me.

A Quick Note on Shame

Shame gets sneaky because it tries to shape what you **are**, not the situation you're in. It doesn't just say, "That wasn't your best moment." It says, "*You are a mess. You are a failure. You are not enough.*" And when you're already tired or maxed out, that voice can feel like the truth. But here's what I've learned: shame shows up when my actions or reactions don't line up with what *I* actually value. Not what I was *taught* to value. Not what the world claps for. What *actually matters* to me.

And instead of ignoring it or trying to prove it wrong, I pause and listen. Not to agree with it. But to understand what triggered it. Did I lash out because I was exhausted and didn't ask for help? Did I say yes when I meant no? Did I show up in a way that didn't feel like me?

Okay. Now I know. Now I can adjust.

That's what shame is trying to tell me, not that I *am* wrong, but that something *felt* wrong. That I crossed my own line somewhere. And when I can name that without spiraling, I get to choose a different response next time.

So I don't shove shame down. But I don't let it run the show either. I use it as a checkpoint. I acknowledge it. And I move forward with a little more clarity and a little less self-judgment.

That's not self-help speak. That's just learning.

***

Now? I'm quicker to catch it. It still creeps in, but I'm better at spotting the signs, like when I start over-explaining or obsessing over a single booking. That's usually my cue to pause and ask, "Is this helping?" And most of the time, the answer is still no. But now, I don't need to spiral to get there. I can stop earlier. That's the shift. That's what this tool is about.

Once again, awareness is a huge element here. You have to catch yourself in the spiral. You must understand when this is happening AND why. What is happening in your life at that moment? Have you been taking care of yourself? Have you been allowing yourself time for rest? Self-care? I know what you're thinking..."But Melissa, how can I have time for rest and self-care when I am literally drowning here?" I get it. I've been there. This is the lesson I fight repeatedly. I assure myself that "I'm good" over and over until I snap. I needed to start seeing the signs before I fell into the spiral. Koko can see it coming from a mile away and often tries to get ahead of it. But let's be honest, I'm stubborn. Part of my problem is, when I feel like I'm in flow, I will resist anything that tries to pull me away from it. I don't see it as the spiral it is. I feel like I'm in control... until I'm not.

A Personal Example

I know I mentioned it before, but I get insanely stubborn when I *think* I'm in flow. Even if that "flow" is actually burnout I'm not aware of. That kind of fake productivity that *looks* shiny from the outside, but inside you're running on fumes and personal expectation?

I'll swear I'm fine. I'll load up my schedule like I'm trying to win some invisible gold medal in over functioning. And if I'm being honest? Sometimes I don't even know I'm spiraling until I'm *deep* in it.

It honestly pains me to admit that Koko always sees it before I do. He'll throw out a soft, "Hey, maybe chill for a second?" And I'll smile like a liar and say, "Nah, I'm good," then go back to whatever project I'm convinced needs to be done at that moment. One day, I'm doing the dishes. I was exhausted (though I couldn't see it). You know that kind of exhaustion where your body is buzzing but your brain feels like it's wading through mud?

My jaw is tight and clenching. I'm replaying the same five stressful thoughts on a loop. And out of nowhere I feel it hit. That *spiral* creeping in.

Right then, in the middle of scrubbing a pan, I hear it: **"Is this helpful?"**

And it wasn't. None of it was. The rushing. The pressure. The performative hustle I keep trying to convince myself is necessary. So I did something I *never* let myself do mid-task: I dropped the sponge. Dried my hands. Walked out of the kitchen. (Yes, I abandoned something mid-task, definitely not something I'm known for.) Sat on the couch. And asked my husband Koko, "Can we start a new show?"

I picked *The Serpent Queen*. (I love period pieces and a good power plot.) It was the perfect choice, something completely unrelated to my to-do list. It was indulgent. It was *rest*. And not the kind I could talk myself out of. Not "I'll just scroll for five minutes" rest. Not "I should be productive while I relax" rest. This was intentional, soul-level, "I am allowed to stop" rest. The kind I hadn't given myself in *way too long*. (and let's be honest, I love a good excuse to binge watch a show, but I rarely *ever* let myself do that.)

And no, the world didn't fall apart. The dishes didn't revolt. I didn't spiral. I didn't fall down the mental staircase that I usually trip face-first down.

Because I paused. I checked myself. And I chose different.

That's the work. Not the perfect schedule. Not the hyper-productivity. Not pushing through just to collapse later.

Just the pause. Just the question. Just the reminder, that little nudge from yourself, **"Hey, this isn't helping."** And the power to walk away anyway. So, next time the spiral starts, pay attention to how it shows up.

Is it in your chest? Do your shoulders tighten? Do you start avoiding people? Snapping at your kids? Do you suddenly need to clean your whole house or check your email for the fiftieth time?

Your body knows the spiral before your brain admits it. So pay attention. Interrupt the pattern. Your spiral usually starts when your soul's been asking for rest, and you keep ignoring her.

"Was that helpful?" No? Then change something. Say no. Go outside. Move your body. Drink some damn water. Touch grass. Literally.

Then breathe. Turn around on that staircase. One step back toward yourself.

***

So, how do we become aware of the spiral? Let's look at this like a science experiment. We have our control, and then we have our variables.

The Control: Your baseline state of awareness. This is your "normal" when you aren't overwhelmed or stressed. Where you are content and calm. It's really important to know what that looks like for you, so you can recognize when things are falling out of alignment.

The Variables: Your triggers. Your signs. These can look different for everyone. They may be physical, emotional, or behavioral signs. Pay attention to how it manifests for you. Where do you feel it in your body? Do you feel headachy? Irritable? Are you avoiding tasks? Are you refusing rest because you've convinced yourself that if you stop now, it'll never get done?

When you start feeling that familiar tug of stress or self-doubt, pause. This moment of reflection can make all the difference.

The Spiral

Close your eyes and imagine yourself standing at the top of a spiral staircase. Each thought, stressor, or unspoken pressure pulls you down one more step. The air gets heavier as you descend; more reactive, more overwhelmed, more disconnected from your baseline. But then, you become aware. And... you pause. You look up. You remember that there is an upstairs. This is where you ask: **"Is this helpful?"** Not to shame yourself. Not to fix it immediately. But to stop the descent. Think of that question as your handrail. It steadies you. It reminds you that you don't have to keep spiraling. You can turn around. One step at a time.

I'm lucky enough to have several people in my orbit that support me. Whether it's your partner, your parents, a trusted friend, or a colleague, having someone who can gently (or not-so-gently if you're stubborn like me) point out when you're heading into a spiral can be incredibly valuable.

Self-Care is non-negotiable. This is a big one. I know it's hard to prioritize self-care when you feel like you're drowning, but it's essential. Think of self-care as the lifeboat that keeps you afloat. Without it, you're more likely to sink into the spiral. So, make time for rest, relaxation, and activities that rejuvenate you.

Incorporate habits that promote mental well-being. This could be meditation, exercise, journaling, or even something as simple as taking a few deep breaths. Get outside. Seriously. Put your feet in the grass. Breathe in the fresh air. Listen to the birds. These practices can help you stay grounded and more aware of your mental state. Sometimes it's hard to see that you're drowning until you try to come up for air. It's more difficult to recover when you reach this point, so really try to be aware of the signs.

Set Boundaries. Learn to say no. This can be one of the hardest lessons, especially if you're used to being a people-pleaser or feel responsible for everything and everyone. But setting boundaries is essential for maintaining your mental health. "Put on your oxygen mask FIRST, then help those around you." You won't do yourself any favors if your mental state is suffering.

Lastly, celebrate your progress, no matter how small. Each time you catch yourself in a spiral and manage to disrupt it, give yourself credit. Acknowledge the effort it takes to change ingrained habits and celebrate those victories. It's a big deal.

Other Helpful Steps

- **Mindfulness and meditation.** Practicing mindfulness or meditation daily can help maintain baseline awareness and reduce the impact of stressors.

- **Schedule breaks for yourself.** Taking regular breaks throughout the day can prevent overwhelm and help maintain focus.

- **Positive self-talk.** Replacing negative thoughts with positive affirmations can disrupt the spiral and boost mood.

- **Physical activity.** Physical activity can help release built-up tension and improve mood. Even walks, yoga, or playing with your kids. Personally, I coach youth soccer and play in a women's over 30 soccer league, I play kickball, and I try to play with the kids. I just recently started at a gym taking 30-minute HIIT classes. These are all things that I never thought I would be able to do.

- **Connect with others.** Find a community of like minds.

Remember, this is a continuous process. It will constantly ebb and flow. Keep experimenting, reflecting, and adjusting as needed.

Reflection:

- What does your inner spiral look like? How does it show up in your body, your thoughts, your habits?

- When was the last time you asked yourself, "Is this helpful?"

- What were you doing, thinking, or believing today that might *seem* productive but is actually keeping you stuck?

- What would it look like to choose gentleness instead of judgment when you catch yourself in a spiral?

- What tiny shift could you make today that would help you feel 5% more grounded?

This isn't about perfection. It's about awareness. It's about not letting the spiral eat you alive. When you ask, *"Is this helpful?"*, you begin to clear the mental clutter. You pause the spiral. You become aware. Because once you learn to pause, once you learn to hold your own damn hand and ask, **"Was that helpful?"**...everything shifts. That question cuts through the noise. It doesn't fix it all. But it opens a crack. And sometimes, that crack is all you need.

Of course, there are times where awareness alone isn't enough. Sometimes you still need a decision-making compass. A way to know if something is right (or wrong) *for you*, even if it's right for everyone else.

That's where the next tool comes in. Because after you disrupt the spiral, the next question becomes: **"Does this give me energy... or take it away?"**

CHAPTER FOUR

DOES THIS BRING ME ENERGY OR TAKE MY ENERGY?

L et's talk about energy for a second. And no, I don't mean calories or caffeine or how many hours of sleep you got last night. I'm talking *real* energy. The invisible kind, but tangible kind. The kind you feel in your gut before your brain can make sense of it.

In the spiritual realm, energy is more than physical force...it's your **life force**. It's runs through you, surrounds you, and connects you to everything and everyone. It's your vibe, your frequency, your fuel. And every single thing you do either feeds it... or depletes it. Think of it as an invisible thread that ties together our mental, emotional, and spiritual states.

The way this tool works is simple. You are given a scenario, and you aren't sure how you feel about it or if you should do it. You're going to ask yourself, "Does this bring me energy or take my energy?" If it brings you energy, you are going to feel excited and feel the need to lean into it. If you struggle with it, dread it, or just feel like you can't bring yourself joyfully to it, that alone should give you the answers you are looking for. Sometimes we don't realize how out of alignment we are until we're too deep in it to feel our own edges.

Enter Crystal.

Crystal and I met at a wedding expo. We were both photographers and gearing up for another expo to help get our names out there. Typically, if I'm honest, I struggle talking to other people - especially photographers. At this time, I had too many previous...let's just say "poor" experiences talking to other photographers. Crystal was different though. Something about her energy drew me in. We became acquaintances and had casual conversations via Facebook messenger here and there. We connected over photography. She is also a mom of three and our conversations were always pretty polite at first. I admired her. She is an *artist* in every sense of the word. She lived about an hour and a half from me. We did each other's family photos that year and that was really the spark of our family's intertwined friendship.

As time went on, we would pop in from time to time just to check in. It wouldn't be until Covid hit that we found ourselves craving connection and someone else who understood the struggles we were facing. That was the beginning of our regular Facetime chats. Our friendship grew and became more and more honest. She was a little bit of a hippie and I really admired the way she lived her life. I had no idea how much she would impact my life moving forward. We would talk about real, deep shit. We would trade off giving advice and holding each other's hands through hard times. During one particularly rough season, she brought me this tool and it has become one of my most valued tools I have. It was sometime around 2022. I was struggling with life's demands. Once again I had overloaded my schedule. She was always there to throw perspective at me. We really thrive on leaving out the niceties with each other. It's one of my favorite things about our friendship.

I remember a stretch of months where I was doing all the things; work, kids, photoshoots, social media, life-but none of it felt right. It wasn't burnout in the traditional sense. I wasn't totally depleted. I was just... dulled. I couldn't explain it. I wasn't sad, but I wasn't lit up either. It was like my whole life was operating on low battery mode. I had said yes to a lot of things I was "supposed to" say yes to. Business opportunities. Family events. Volunteer roles. Coaching responsibilities. All good things. But none of them felt aligned.

They felt obligatory. Necessary. And when you start living from necessity instead of energy, your soul begins to shut down quietly. You become a function instead of a force.

I was struggling and during one of our calls, she challenged me, "Who told you this was the life you had to maintain?" And with that, I realized, I was running at a pace that wasn't mine. Following a map that wasn't mine. Saying yes to things that didn't feed me because I thought that's what good people do. What responsible people do. What strong women do.

But being strong doesn't mean being drained. And alignment doesn't necessarily mean ease, but it does mean honesty. Crystal encouraged me to start figuring out how to reign things in. She called it a filter. "Does this bring me energy, or does this take my energy". And there it was. That tool (or filter) changed my life. I took it a step further and started listing out my daily responsibilities. I call it inventory.

It may be beneficial to take inventory of what you have in your life currently. I'm talking top to bottom. Start with your morning routine and work your way throughout the day. This is a good time to figure out what is aligning with your values and where you need work. Trust me, we all need work. Once we can identify what parts of your life need adjusting, it starts a ripple effect. Remember, this is all a part of healing and you may find some uncomfortable areas pop up.

You may find that your job is draining your energy. It might be your family. It could be overbooking yourself.

The best thing you can do here is to be honest with yourself. So what do you do when you find that something is taking your energy?

Good question, and ultimately, this depends on what kind of life you want to live. This is not easy. Healing is typically coupled with pain and you have to be willing to do the work.

I'd like you to take a moment and inventory. I want you to make a list (or find this chapter four in the workbook). Center this list on the paper and write down the constants of your life. What does a typical day look like for you? Who do you see? Try to be as detailed as possible.

This is what it might look like:
Inventory Example

Daily Activities:

Alarm / snooze / snuggle kitty
Wake up
Find morning affirmation to kick off the day
Feed the meow
Turn on music
Shower
Cannabis work (I work in the industry, too)
MDB work
Lunch with Koko
Emails
Get kids from school
Connect with kids
Dinner / drive-thru
Sports
Gym
Garage
Bed

People:

Person A
Person B
Person C
Person D

Once you have your typical day listed, I want you to label the top of the paper. On the left side, write "TAKE." On the right side, write "GIVE."

Now, go through your inventory and categorize each item: Does it take your energy, or does it give you energy?

Remember: This Isn't Judgment, It's Awareness

Recognizing the sources of your energy and the drains on it is a crucial step in aligning your life with your true self. Once you have your list divided, you can begin to make more conscious choices about where to spend your time and energy.

Energy, in the spiritual sense, is often referred to as chi, prana, or life force. It is the unseen power that animates all living things.

When our energy is balanced and flowing freely, we feel vibrant, healthy, and connected to our higher self and the world around us. When it's blocked or depleted, we may experience:

- Physical illness

- Emotional distress

- A sense of disconnection

Spiritual practices like meditation, yoga, and Reiki are designed to balance and enhance this energy flow. These tools help clear blockages and allow life force to move through you again, promoting healing and well-being.

By asking yourself "Does this give me energy or take it away?" you're tuning into your spiritual energy flow. Activities and people that give you energy align with your higher self. Those that drain it? They're blocking your path.

Where This Tool Is Most Powerful: The Pause Before the Yes

You might be using this tool to reflect on what's already draining you... your schedule, your habits, your relationships. That's good. That's a solid starting point. We need to know what's costing us our peace on a daily basis. But the moment this tool becomes a *life-changer* is when you use it **before** you say yes.

Before you agree to take on a new project. Before you volunteer. Before you commit out of guilt, flattery, or habit.

That's the real moment. The pause. We don't protect our energy in hindsight; we protect it in the moment we decide. Honestly, that's where most of us get it wrong. We get caught in the swirl, the autopilot yes, the obligatory yes, the desire to be helpful, liked, needed, seen. And then we feel bitter or buried later, wondering why we're so damn exhausted.

Let me say this clearly: **Energy protection is a before-the-fact practice.**

If you've never given yourself permission to slow down and check in before responding, this is your cue to start. I have a paper calendar at home for this exact reason. Not because I'm old school (okay, I am), but because it slows me down. It allows me a built-in pause. It keeps me from saying yes too quickly.

When someone asks me if I'm free, I get to say, *"Let me check when I get home."* That sentence gives me space. It gives me room to sit with it. To look ahead and ask: **What will this take from me? What will I have to give up for this?**

Because the truth is, just because it fits into the calendar, doesn't mean it fits into the life you're trying to build.
Read that last line again.

Maybe that event *technically* works on Thursday night, but if Thursday nights are usually your wind-down time with your kids, or when you need to reset your nervous system, then nope, it *doesn't* fit.

Every yes is an energy transaction. But also, please remember, every yes is also a quiet no to something else. A no to something that may be the *thing* you've been hoping for. So, use this tool in the moment. Use it **before** you offer up your time, your energy, your presence.

Use it to ask:

- Will this give me energy or take it?

- Will this align with what I'm fighting for?

- Will this future version of me thank me or resent me?

We don't owe anyone the version of us who says yes out of fear. We protect the version of us who's learning to choose with intention. And if you're not sure yet? Pause. That's reason enough to wait. You don't need to decide on the spot. You're not rude for giving yourself time to think about it. You don't need to shrink or shape-shift. You need to **check in** with your body and your bandwidth.

The clearest answers usually show up when you give them a second to arrive.

This doesn't mean everything that takes energy is bad, some things are necessary, even meaningful. But if your life is built mostly of takers, it's time to restructure.

Understanding and managing your energy is a powerful tool in your healing journey. It enables you to create a life that supports your well-being and aligns with your true self. So, take this inventory seriously. This is a step toward a more conscious, balanced, and fulfilling life.

Once you become aware of what gives and takes your energy, the next step is choosing how to respond. Awareness is powerful, but it's what you do with that awareness that creates change.

Sometimes, even after you've identified the drains and made the adjustments, life still throws you into moments that feel chaotic or heavy. You can't always eliminate every energy taker. You still have bills to pay, kids to care for, jobs to show up for. But you can meet those moments with intention.

And that's where the next tool comes in. Because even when you've cleared your schedule, protected your peace, and aligned your energy... there will be days when it still feels hard. There will be foggy mornings and loud afternoons and moments where it all feels like too much again. And when that happens? You ask yourself:

"What am I fighting for?"

CHAPTER FIVE

WHAT AM I FIGHTING FOR?

This next tool was a gem dropped by Crystal during one of our usual "pretending-not-to-be-therapy-even-though-it's-totally-therapy" chats. I don't even think she realizes how impactful she is...she just casually drops soul-splitting wisdom like she's passing the salt. I wanted this tool right after the last one because I use them together like a left hook and a grounding hand. They work. They *bring me back*.

"What am I fighting for?" is one of my go-to lifelines. When I feel untethered, overwhelmed, spiraling...I ask it. Not because I always know the answer. But because the asking itself brings me back to solid ground. It doesn't demand perfection. It doesn't expect you to have some pristine vision board ready to go. It just asks you to remember: *Why are you still in it?*

It's the question I reach for when I catch myself brushing off my kids' stories. When I snap too fast. When I lose presence and it breaks my damn heart, because *that's not who I want to be.* That's not what I'm fighting for.

You'll find this question showing up in the middle of tears, in the aftermath of overreacting, in the in-between moment before your next bad decision. When everything feels like too much (or not enough) ask it:

What am I fighting for?

And sometimes? You won't know. The fog is thick. The day is loud. The doubt is louder. But even *asking* gives you something to grip. A thread. A breath. A pause. It's another handrail on the spiral staircase. And sometimes, that's enough. It reminds you you're *still* fighting, even if the words haven't caught up yet.

First, Admit You're in a Fight

Let's be real...life is full of fights. Big ones. Silent ones. Invisible ones that don't even show up in words, just in headaches, short tempers, and that low-grade hum of anxiety you can't shake.

The first move? **Admit you're in it.**

Ask yourself: What's making everything feel so heavy? What external noise or internal chaos is pushing me to the edge? What am I ignoring that's been begging for attention? Sometimes it's obvious. But sometimes it's buried under a week of overstimulation, 16 "I'm fine"s, and a calendar full of commitments that don't actually serve you.

This isn't a deep-dive journal prompt. This is the *pull-you-out-of-the-quicksand* kind of tool. It's the rope. Use it when your thoughts feel like they're drowning you.

Ask:

- Am I fighting to stay present for my kids?

- Am I fighting for my own damn peace?

- Am I just fighting to get through this *one* wild moment without snapping?

That counts. That's enough. You don't need a mission statement...just a flicker of clarity. A sliver of "why" to hold onto.

Scene Check: You Know This One

You're mid-chaos. Work is relentless. The house is loud. The to-do list is a scroll that never ends. You skipped lunch...again. You're short-tempered. You're overstimulated. You're on the verge of snapping (or let's be honest, maybe you already did.)

Let's Pause.

Let's Breathe.

Let's ask the damn question.

What am I fighting for?

Maybe it's to protect your peace. Maybe it's to model something better for your kids. Maybe it's just to prove to yourself that you don't have to keep unraveling like this. We've got this.

 ### Visualization Exercise:

Close your eyes and imagine you're standing in a foggy forest. You can't see even two feet in front of you. The air is thick. The path is unclear. Everything feels gray and heavy. It's disorienting.

Now imagine a bright-colored cord tied gently around your wrist. It trails behind you...back through the fog, to something safe. Something real. Something that matters.

Maybe it's your kids. Maybe it's your peace. Maybe it's the woman you're still becoming.

That cord is your **why**.

When the fog thickens and when you can't see the next step, reach for that cord. Let the question "What am I fighting for?" guide you back to what's real.

More Ways to Stay Grounded (Other Grounding Tools When the Fight Gets Loud)

This question works best when paired with nervous system support. When your body feels like a battleground, give it reinforcements.

Mindfulness, but Make It Useful. You don't need to chant affirmations on a mountaintop. Just get still for two minutes. Stretch. Put your feet in the grass (that's kinda my personal go-to, can you tell?!). Light a candle. Name what you see. Feel your body. Remember you *exist*—you're not just reacting.

Simple Breath Reset:

- Inhale for 4

- Hold for 4

- Exhale for 6 Repeat until you feel the edge dull a little. You're not broken. You're just maxed out. Breathe like it matters.

Bonus Support: Tapping (A Quick Note)

Let's talk about *tapping*—also called EFT. Not because I'm an expert (I'm certainly not), but because this simple tool *actually worked* when I needed it most. (This is just my personal experience with this. I'm sure there are other methods.)

I first tried it at a holiday gathering where I was to simply introduce myself in front of a group of women I didn't know. My heart was pounding. My palms were sweating. (Cue: full body panic mode) I was two seconds from saying "No thank you" and walking out. I managed to get through it. My voice was shaky. I was embarrassed. Even thinking of it now makes me full body cringe. This was just an introduction. How hard is it to say, "Hey, I'm Melissa, and I'm a boudoir photographer"?! Well...apparently for me, really hard. The room felt like it was closing in. My body surged with heat. I don't even remember what was asked or what else I said. They continued around the room.

One of the women, an EMDR therapist, caught my attention and though I was wildly nervous, I sought her out after our introductions. She was a warm soul, one of those that you instantly feel at ease with. After we talked for a moment and I teased about my anxieties, she asked, gently, "Want to try something?" I nervously agreed. (She must have known I was a mess) We sat on the floor. I was concerned the others would think I was crazy - but surrendered (which was something new for me, too!). This was brought to me. I knew it would be a gift. She had me close my eyes and focus on my breathing. She had me cross my arms and start tapping rhythmically on each bicep. Tap. Tap. Tap.

Tap. Tap. Tap. Tap. Inhale 2, 3, 4... Hold 2, 3, 4... Exhale 2, 3, 4, 5, 6... Repeat.

It worked. I'm still kind of mad about how well it worked. How could something so simple be so effective? That moment taught me something: **Regulation doesn't have to be loud. It doesn't have to be perfect. It just has to work.**

You can try it when:

- You feel like you're about to lose it

- You're prepping for something hard

- You feel the spiral starting

(There are tons of tutorials out there. Find one. Try it. Or don't. Just find *something* that helps you come home to yourself.) Then use it. No apology needed.

Reflection

Take a few minutes and journal through any of these:

- What is one thing I'm currently fighting for, even if I haven't said it out loud?

- When was the last time I felt disconnected from my *why*?

- What signs does my body give me when I'm off-center?

- What's one moment from this week I wish I had paused and asked this question?

- What kind of person am I trying to be, and what's worth fighting for in her name?

"What am I fighting for?" doesn't always give you an immediate or perfect answer.

But it opens the door. It cracks the fog. It reminds you that you don't need to have it all figured out to keep moving with intention. You're not just reacting, you're remembering. You're not just surviving, you're choosing. And the next time you feel yourself unraveling, ask the question. Then breathe. And pull on the cord. You're still in the fight, and that means something. And if no answer comes? That's okay too. You pause, you breathe, you pull anyway.

That's when the work shifts from action to attention. From the noise around you to the whisper within. Because the next battle? It might not be the calendar or the chaos.

It might be the voice in your own head.

And that's where we go next.

Chapter Six

Mirror Talk and Mantras

S ometimes, the fight isn't about action, it's about voice. It's about how we speak to ourselves when the world goes quiet. It's about what we say in the mirror after the breakdown. Because sometimes, what we're really fighting for is a softer way to speak to ourselves. I used to roll my eyes at affirmations. They felt fake. Forced. Like slapping glitter on a cracked foundation. Or like trying to duct tape a soul back together and hoping no one notices it's still bleeding underneath.

Because how the hell was I supposed to say "I am enough" when I didn't believe it? When I felt like I was failing at everything and the only thing I was "enough" at was imagining the worst-case scenario? My brain didn't need help being negative. I was already fluent in disaster planning. I could feel a tiny shift in tone from someone I loved and spiral into an entire rejection arc in 0.3 seconds.
"I'm failing."
"I'm too much."
"I'm not enough."
"I'm not beautiful."
"I'm forgettable."

Not forgetful like "oops, where are my keys?" Forgettable as in, others don't remember I'm here.

I've been the person who shows up fully and still feels invisible. I've poured into people, supported them, stayed steady, kind, present, and watched them overlook me like I never existed. Like I wasn't remarkable enough to stick. So, when I tried to say things like "I am beautiful" or "I am worthy," or "I am enough", I didn't feel powerful. I felt pathetic. I literally scoffed at myself the first time I said it. Because it felt like lying. Because it felt like pretending I mattered in a world that hadn't confirmed it back to me. But some part of me still whispered, "Try again." So I said it again. Not because I believed it, but because I wanted to. And sometimes, *wanting* is enough to start. Then something strange started to happen. The hatred in my head got quieter (still there, but not as loud). I didn't immediately rip myself apart in every photo. I didn't spiral as hard every time someone was distant.

I started to ask myself: What are the facts?

I started using tools, like the color grounding technique when anxiety hit me heavy or if I started spiraling.
Find 5 red things.
4 blue.
3 green.
2 black.
1 brown.
It pulled me out of the storm and into the room. It reminded me my thoughts are not always telling the truth.

And slowly, the mantras stopped sounding like lies. They started sounding like possibilities.

Some days, it still feels like a lie. This isn't about toxic positivity or pretending you're healed. It's about planting seeds that grow into truth. Some days you'll say the mantra and mean it. Some days you'll say it through tears. Some days it'll sound like sarcasm, and you'll feel ridiculous. But say it anyway. Especially then.
"I am beautiful."
"I am visible."
"I am someone people remember."
"Even when others overlook me, I see myself."
"I matter, even in the quiet."

That's where it starts. This work isn't loud. It isn't public. It happens in stolen moments, before bed, after tears, while brushing your teeth, right before you break. Mantras are tiny revolutions you stage in the quietest places. They aren't just words. They're interruptions and invitations. They stop the spiral. They soften the inner critic. They interrupt the generational echoes of shame and smallness and not-enough-ness.

I am beautiful
I am worthy
I am enough

They're tiny acts of rebellion against everything you've been taught to believe about your worth. Every time you speak a mantra, you're not just whispering to yourself, you're rewiring yourself. You're literally creating new grooves in your brain, new defaults that weren't there before. And the more we do it, the stronger the path becomes. It's stepping off the path and creating your own, new path. At first, it feels unnatural and uncomfortable. Like walking through tall grass where no one's walked before. You're swatting away old thoughts like branches. The ground is uneven. You're not sure where it's leading. And there's a part of you that wants to turn around and go back to the worn trail, the one paved by old beliefs, family patterns, cultural conditioning. The one you know how to navigate. But every time you repeat a mantra, you press your foot down a little firmer on the new path. Every time you choose kindness instead of criticism, the grass bends. The way becomes more visible. More familiar. More yours. Eventually, it doesn't feel like forging a path anymore. **It feels like coming home.**

And one day, you'll look back and realize you're not just walking it, you've built it. A path lined with grace and gentleness and with self-trust.

And maybe, just maybe, someone else will follow behind you and feel less alone because you cleared the way. And that's what healing is. Not just the big cathartic moments. But the tiny, quiet, intentional repetitions that rewire who we think we are. Because if you've spent years calling yourself a failure, a burden, too much, or not enough, of course kindness will feel like a foreign language.

That's why we repeat it. Even when it feels like a lie. Even when it sounds fake. Even when it makes your skin crawl. You're teaching your body what safety sounds like. You're practicing. You're reminding your nervous system that not every mirror moment has to be an attack.

Mantras are important because they:

- Create a pause in emotional reactivity

- Calm the nervous system through repetition

- Anchor us in a new identity (even when the old one fights back)

- Offer something to reach for when logic and therapy and coping tools fall short

- Become a spiritual tether in moments when your worth feels like it's slipping

Picture the mirror, not as a judge, but as a portal. One that doesn't show you your flaws. One that reflects your *becoming*. Not what you are supposed to be. But what you already are, just underneath the dust, the doubt, the noise. Let your mirror become a place of re-entry. Where you try again. Where you say the words that feel ridiculous. Where you meet yourself where you are, and speak to where you're going.

Want to take this further?

Here's your challenge. Write one mantra on a sticky note. Stick it to your mirror. Say it out loud - yes out loud - **every day for the next 7 days**. Even if you roll your eyes. Even if you just mouth it. Even if you cry halfway through. My personal favorite is: "I am beautiful, I am worthy, I am enough" You don't need to believe it yet. You just need to *want* to believe it. That's the seed that will eventually blossom.

Other mantras that have stayed with me:

- I am allowed to be both a masterpiece and a work in progress.

- I am allowed to rest.

- My worth isn't something I prove. It's something I own.

- I am safe to be seen, even if no one claps for me.

- I do not have to shrink to be loved.

- I remember who I am, even when others don't.

- We don't do that anymore (of course!)

Let your voice become the one that speaks kindness when no one else does. Let it be your anchor, your reminder, your protector, your comeback and your return.

***

Want to take this even deeper? I do something that might sound intense, but it helps bring me back to what matters. I imagine a world where I'm no longer here. And I ask, what do my kids have as reminders of me? What beautiful things will they see in the photos I used to hate? What will I leave behind for them to love... if I'm no longer here? That's when I stop picking myself apart. That's when I remember: **my body is part of their memory of me.** Not because of how it looked, but because of the way it loved. Don't get me wrong. I'm not perfect at this, nor am I claiming to be. There are times that I still falter. But it is getting easier.

I think of my mom. She struggled with her body her whole life. She believed she had to be perfectly thin to be worthy. And as a teen, she was a competitive swimmer. Thin. Powerful. But after pregnancy, when her body changed, something in her belief system broke.

She couldn't accept what her body became. She couldn't see the beauty I always saw in her.

She missed out on so many photos, on so many moments, because she didn't feel confident enough to exist in them imperfectly. The few I have of her from my childhood? She's usually holding up a hand to block the camera. Hiding. Erasing. Protecting something she'd learned to be ashamed of.

But I didn't see her body. I saw *her*. The one who scooped me up every time I fell. The one who showed up. The one who made me feel safe in a world that often didn't. I wish, for a moment, she could see herself the way I see her.

And now... I'm the mom. I catch myself saying things like "I'm getting fat" or "Ugh, I hate the way this looks on me." I'll be honest, (sorry, Mom), but it's *her* voice. It's how she talked about herself. It's how I learned to see my body. Because even though I saw her as perfect and enough, her words taught me something different. They taught me that even the women I admired most could still hate themselves out loud. That beauty wasn't what you *were*, it was something you had to earn, and if you didn't meet the mark, you stayed quiet. You shrunk. You hid from the camera. You laughed it off.

Her voice became the one I used on myself. Until I started passing it on. Unintentionally. Invisibly. Until my daughter heard me and said, "Stop talking about yourself like that." Worse (or better), she calls me out. She wasn't just annoyed. She was *hurt*. And I don't blame her. She doesn't want to watch me disappear from my own life or existing in memories the way I watched my mom do it. She sees me the way I saw *her*, as beautiful, warm, enough. Always.

Because to her, I *am* enough. I'm her mom. Her safe place. Her favorite face. And every time I tear myself apart, I'm teaching her how to do the same. I'm showing her what it looks like to disappear in real time. To erase yourself before anyone else gets the chance.

And she sees my healing. She sees me trying to love myself and failing sometimes. (Okay, more than sometimes) But she also sees me trying again. And I hope that's what sticks.

And that's the moment where it hits. I'm not just healing for me. It's for her. It's for the girl I used to be. It's for my mom, my aunt, and my grandma. I'm healing to break the pattern. To make sure she never learns to dim her light to feel lovable. To make sure she stays in the picture. We don't do mantras to fake it. We do them to remember. To rewrite. To stay in the frame. We do them to leave something behind, besides shame.

Say it again. Say it anyway. Because the moment you start speaking to yourself with kindness... the noise might actually get louder. Not quieter. And that's where most people stop. But not you.

You're here.

And if you're brave enough to speak to yourself differently, then you're ready for what comes next:

Stillness. Not the kind they sell you in meditation apps. Not the soft, candlelit version with lavender and perfect posture. I mean the kind that cracks you open.

That brings the truth you've been avoiding straight to the surface. The kind of quiet that doesn't calm you, it confronts you.

Because the moment you stop hiding from your voice, you start hearing everything else. Let's go there.

CHAPTER SEVEN

MINDFULNESS

M indfulness gets romanticized like it's all bath bombs and serenity. But let's be real: sometimes, mindfulness wrecks you. It doesn't soothe, nope, it exposes. It pulls back the curtain on everything you've been too busy to feel. You slow down and expect calm, but instead, you find the chaos you've been avoiding. That ache in your chest you couldn't name? That intrusive thought you brushed off? That thing that triggered you three days ago but got stuffed under "I don't have time"?

Stillness brings it all back. And if you're not ready for that, you might think you're doing something wrong. That your brain's too broken for peace. That mindfulness isn't "working." But, I promise you, it is. You're not broken. You're just finally quiet enough to hear what's real.

When I first started "being more mindful," I thought I'd feel calm. Grounded. More patient, even. What I got instead? Hah. Rage I hadn't let myself feel. Sadness I didn't want to name. Shame I thought I'd healed. Thought spirals I assumed were just "how my brain works."

I remember trying to do mindfulness the "right" way, you know, cross-legged on the floor, palms up like every Pinterest post told me. Instead, my back hurt. My brain raced. I sat there questioning myself. *This is supposed to help?*

I wasn't healing. I was performing peace because I thought that's what growth looked like.

I tried yoga. I wasn't great at it, but it gave me an outlet. It wasn't until I dropped into child's pose (head down, arms stretched out, vulnerable as hell) that something finally shifted. Not because I was doing it "right," but because I stopped pretending. I let go of the performance. I was able to *be* in that moment.

Stillness didn't always bring calm. Sometimes it brought tears. Sometimes truth. And honestly, sometimes depression.

I've slipped into depressive states before, when movement feels impossible, presence feels fake, and my worth feels microscopic. But I don't fight it anymore. Now? I lean in. Not because I like it, but because I've learned to ask:

What is this here to teach me?
What haven't I healed?
What is this moment trying to surface?

I don't collapse in it anymore. I get *curious* inside it. I look around. I bask in it until the answers start to reveal themselves. And when I don't get mindful (when I avoid stillness) I spiral faster. I forget who I am. My joy disappears. My softness goes quiet.

Every time I've tried to spiritually bypass the hard stuff, the Universe shows up with a full-on cosmic takedown. At a certain point, the Universe stops operating in subtlety. It gave you the hints that you needed to shift. It nudged you along the path. But if you ignore it, you're going to be in for a rude awakening. You'll get body slammed. Held down. Forced to look at what you didn't want to see.

It's never pretty. But it's always necessary. And eventually (thankfully) it's freeing.

A 30-Second Reset (Try This)

If you're in it right now, if the quiet is getting loud I want you to try this:

Put your hand on your chest. Inhale for 4... hold for 4... exhale for 6. Name one emotion you're feeling. Just one. Sit with it. Don't fix it. Just notice. Feel where it manifests in your body. Be aware.

That's it. That's mindfulness, too.

If mindfulness has ever made you feel worse instead of better... you're not alone. And when it cracks you open, when it dredges up all the things you've stuffed down or spiritualized away, what comes next matters just as much.

Because stillness reveals, but filters protect...and tools help you manage.

These are the small practices that have helped me stay connected when things get loud:

- Know that discomfort doesn't mean danger. Just because a feeling is loud doesn't mean it's unsafe. I sit with it. I breathe through it. I ask: *Is this mine? Is this now? Is this true?*

- Set a timer, not an expectation. Forget the 30-minute "perfect" meditation. Sometimes five minutes of breathing is all I have. Sometimes it's one. That counts. That's presence.

- Let it be messy. You don't have to clear your mind. You just have to notice it. When thoughts come up, I name them: *"That's fear." "That's old programming." "That's not mine anymore."* Mindfulness isn't the absence of thoughts. It's the awareness of them.

- Move after you sit. Move any chance you get. Stillness doesn't mean stagnation. Sometimes I shake it out. Dance. Journal. Other times, I play soccer. There's something about running hard, laughing, and losing yourself in strategy. It clears my mind in ways meditation never could. It pulls me into now.

Find that "thing" that allows you no choice but to be present.

I think it's important to note that not all mindfulness looks like meditation. Some of my deepest self-awareness hasn't happened on a mat, it has come in our garage. At night. Sitting on mismatched chairs, talking with Koko. It's where we drop the act. It's where we say the quiet parts out loud. We call it our "universal portal," because something always shifts there. No candles. No mantras. Just truth.

And that's mindfulness, too.

The Velvet Rope

Stillness cracked me open. But what no one warned me about was the *aftershock*. Once the silence did its job, once it unearthed the rage, the sadness, the shame, the world around me didn't quiet down to match.

It actually got louder. The noise didn't stop. It just shifted from internal chaos to external interference.

Suddenly, I could hear it all:

- The projections other people threw at me.

- The passive-aggressive comments that used to slip by unnoticed.

- The guilt-laced expectations.

- The tension in conversations I once dismissed as "just a weird vibe."

When you clear the internal clutter, the external noise becomes unbearable. What used to blend into the background now feels like a fire alarm going off. And you can't un-hear it once you've heard it.

When that happens, you need a filter. A boundary. Or, as I call it... your velvet rope.

Picture this:

You are the bouncer of your own nervous system.

You decide what gets past the velvet rope. Who gets in, who stays outside, and who needs to come back another day...when they're not carrying that chaotic energy with them.

This isn't about judgment. It's about capacity.

Every time I ignore that velvet rope, I pay for it. Not always loudly, but subtly...like a slow leak in a tire. I'm a little more anxious. A little less patient. I show up to the things that matter most already emptied by what didn't.

And sometimes, it's not a person you let past the rope, it's a thought. A doubt. A trigger that dressed itself up as "concern."

A DM That Snuck In

There was a time I opened my DMs after a long, emotionally draining day. I hadn't eaten dinner yet. My shoulders were tight. My head ached. I was already stretched thin and already doubting myself in that low, quiet way you don't always realize until something pushes it deeper.

And there it was.

A message from someone I barely knew. Not cruel or aggressive, but just wrapped in that faux-soft concern that makes you feel like the bad guy for being affected. *"I don't mean this in a bad way, but you've seemed really emotional in your posts lately. Are you sure you're okay putting all that out there?"*

That was it. Two sentences. But it landed like a brick. I reread it five times. Each time, the doubt grew louder. Was I being too much, too vulnerable, too loud in my healing?

I didn't filter it. I let it in. I didn't pause. I didn't ask if it was about me or them. I opened the velvet rope wide and gave it a seat at the table. I didn't just let it in...I served it dinner, poured it wine, and let it narrate my worth.

And then I brought it to dinner with my kids. I was there, but I wasn't *there*. My body sat at the table. My hands passed plates. But my mind was far away, replaying that message, dissecting my tone in old posts, wondering if the person was right. Had I been "oversharing"? Was I embarrassing myself and didn't know it?

I burned the tortillas. I snapped at one of the kids over something small.

It pulled at me while I was tucking them in, my favorite time of night, our bedtime routine, the quiet one-on-one check-in. The laughs and giggles. The playfulness right before bed.

But that night, I rushed it. I turned out the light too quickly, my chest still tight with invisible judgment. Because I had absorbed someone else's projection and allowed it to speak louder than my presence.

It followed me into sleep where I tossed and turned all night. My anxiety was pulsing through me. I woke up with clenched fists and a heavy heart. Already defeated and behind. Like I had failed some invisible test I didn't even know I was taking.

That's the cost of unfiltered living. Not just distraction or hurt feelings, but disconnection from yourself.

And when you're disconnected from yourself, you can't be fully present for anyone, let alone with the people you love. You start showing up guarded. Defensive. Shrinking. Second-guessing everything you were so sure of just a day ago.

That's what one unfiltered moment can do.

And that's why I started building my arsenal of tools and filters, not to push people away, but to protect who I'm becoming.

The Filter Test

Here's how I keep my mind from becoming an emotional landfill:

- "Was that about me? Or them?" A weird tone. A passive-aggressive comment. A vibe shift that used to send me spiraling. Now I ask: Was that about me... or were they just having a moment that had nothing to do with me? Most of the time? It's not about me. And I let it go. (This takes a bit of practice.)

- "Do I need to feel this? Or is this someone else's energy?" As someone who absorbs everything, I have to pause and check in: Did I feel this way before that conversation? Before I walked into that room? Before I opened that app? If not, it's probably not mine. And I don't have to carry it.

- "What am I feeding my mind right now?" We talk about food diets. But what about mental diets? Am I scrolling with intention or out of habit? Am I consuming content that energizes me, or empties me? Is this connection... or comparison? If I wouldn't feed my kids junk every meal, why do I let my brain binge on anxiety?

- "Would I talk to my child like this?" This one hits hard. It's probably my strongest one. When I hear myself spiral, *"You're falling behind,"* *"No one cares,"* *"You're not good enough"*, I have to pause and ask, "Would I ever say this to my child?" If the answer is no... then I don't get to say it to me either. It's not easy, but it's effective.

Filters Change As You Do

What drained you last month might not affect you now. What felt peaceful before might feel heavy today. That doesn't make you inconsistent. It makes you *awake*.

Your filters *should* grow with you.

Your needs change. Your capacity shifts. Your healing deepens.

So your filters and your tools? They're going to evolve too.

Even as I've been writing this, I've realized how much mine have. Some of these filters guided me through a time in my life. I was desperate for them, and now? They aren't my everyday pull.

They're tucked away. Not necessarily gone, but just not needed daily.

Sometimes I mute someone whose content stings a little too close. Weeks later, I unmute. Sometimes I walk away from a convo...not because I'm done forever, but because I don't have the *space* right now.

Filters aren't fixed. They're fluid. Living boundaries. Responsive to who you are *right now.*

You don't need permission to shift what your peace requires. You just need to pay attention and honor it.

Filters don't make you cold. They don't mean you're cutting everyone off. They just mean you're choosing what's allowed to take up space in your mind, your heart, your day.

Because not everything deserves a front-row seat to your nervous system. Think of it like this: your inbox has a spam folder, right? Well, your brain needs one too. There's some thoughts, some people, some energies...spam.

You don't have to open every emotional email. You don't have to click every link someone sends you. You don't even have to reply. You just mark it for what it is and move on. Let your mental space be yours again. Let your energy belong to you.

Reflection:

- What thoughts have I let in recently that don't belong to me?

- Which filter do I need to strengthen right now?

- What energy am I allowing that feels like spam?

- Is there something I've outgrown, but I'm still letting it in, out of habit?

- If my peace had a velvet rope, what would I stop letting in today?

And here's the truth: Sometimes the biggest energy drain in your life isn't a random internet comment or a scroll session. Sometimes...It's a conversation you're not having. A relationship that needs redefining. A boundary that's gone unspoken. A truth you've swallowed so many times it's become a lump in your throat. You can run your filters. You can clear your inbox. You can block, mute, unfollow, and protect your peace like your life depends on it.

But if you're still silencing your truth to keep the peace? You're not free yet.

Which brings us to the next tool and maybe one of the hardest parts of healing:

Having the difficult conversation.

Chapter Eight

Having the Difficult Conversation

You can't keep making yourself smaller just to keep the peace. Peace built on silence isn't peace. It's tension dressed up as tolerance. And it rots you from the inside out. This is the part of healing where most people want to look away. Because having the difficult conversation isn't for the faint of heart. This is where shit gets real. This is where you have to rip off the Band-Aid and say the real thing, regardless of how it's taken. This is where you stop dancing around the tension and walk straight into it. And ya, it's scary. It's uncomfortable. It's messy. But do you know what's worse?

Dragging it out. That's what kills you slowly. We carry these conversations in our bodies before we ever say a word. We imagine how they'll react. We rehearse their lines and plan our comebacks. We try to package the truth in something soft so we're not seen as mean or dramatic or "too much." But the longer we hold onto it, the longer we suffer. You might think you're protecting the relationship, or the other person, or even yourself. But what you're actually doing is sacrificing your peace to avoid discomfort. Your silence has symptoms.

Let me say it straight:

Avoiding the hard conversation does not save you pain. It just stretches it out over time.

I used to over prepare. "If they say this, then I'll say that." "If they get upset, I'll explain it like this." "If they misunderstand, I'll fix it with this version."

That just doesn't work.

Conversations don't follow scripts. They're not predictable. And you're not in control of how someone receives your honesty. All you can do is be brave enough to say what needs to be said. No manipulation. No micromanaging. Just truth. Say it. Clean. Clear. Calm. Say it with love. Say it with boundaries. Say it so your soul stops spinning. Let's be real, your body's not going to love it at first.

Before: You'll feel it. The tension. The weight. The ache in your chest. The pressure in your stomach.
During: Your voice might shake. Your breath might get short. You might want to run.
After: You'll process. Reflect. Maybe cry. Maybe question yourself.

But then?

Relief.

Even when it doesn't go perfectly. Even if the conversation was hard as hell. You'll feel a shift. Because you're not carrying the weight of unspoken truth anymore.

This isn't just about confrontations or breakups or dramatic boundaries.

Some of the hardest conversations are quiet.

- Telling your partner you feel disconnected, even if they haven't done anything "wrong"

- Asking your parent to stop commenting on your body

- Admitting to your child that you overreacted and you're working on it

- Telling a friend you need space, even though you love them

- Saying, "This hurt me," instead of pretending you're fine

They're not explosive. But they're intimate. And that can be even scarier. Because they make you vulnerable in a way yelling never could.

They say:
I care about you enough to be honest.
I care about myself enough to speak up.

There was a moment, one of those quiet, heavy ones, where I had to tell someone I loved deeply that the way we were showing up for each other wasn't working anymore. I wasn't mad. I wasn't angry. I was disappointed. And scared. And exhausted from carrying it all in silence. I sat with it for weeks. I ran the conversation over and over in my head. I was plagued by it. It was eating me. And when I finally said it, it didn't land perfectly. But it landed. We both walked away changed. And I walked away free. That conversation gave me back my energy. It gave me clarity. It let me stop performing, stop pretending, stop hoping they'd just figure it out. The conversation might not fix the dynamic. But it will set you free. And sometimes, that's the only outcome you're responsible for.

One thing I've learned the hard way: Don't project your fear or pain onto the other person.

It's easy to come in hot, you know, defensive, angry, already rehearsing the fight in your head. But that doesn't hold space for the other person's humanity. You can say the hard thing without making them the villain. You can be clear and firm without turning it into a takedown. You can disagree without disconnecting. We hold space for both truths: Yours and theirs. That's what emotional maturity looks like. And that maturity is holding your truth in one hand and someone else's humanity in the other.

You don't need a perfect reason to speak your truth. But here are a few signs it might be time:

- You feel anxious before seeing or talking to them

- You replay the same conversation in your head, over and over

- You're avoiding them or editing yourself around them

- You're smiling while secretly building resentment

- You've said "it's fine" so many times it doesn't even sound like your voice anymore

If something is living rent-free in your mind, **it's costing your peace**. That's reason enough.

When You Don't Have the Conversation

Let's talk about what happens when you don't have the conversation. When you keep holding it in even when you know you need to say something, but you're not there yet. You smile through tension. You say "it's fine" while something eats away at you. You convince yourself you're over it, but it still shows up, in your tone, your body, your energy. You become snappy over small things. You withdraw. You build stories in your head and punish the other person for things they don't even know they did. You start feeling like you're the problem, because you've silenced your truth so long it doesn't even feel real anymore.

Avoiding the conversation doesn't preserve the connection. It poisons it. It turns unspoken words into resentment. It turns compassion into distance. It turns misunderstanding into a slow decay of trust. And worst of all? It costs you. Your peace. Your power. Your presence.

Eventually, the energy it takes to suppress becomes heavier than the discomfort of just saying the damn thing. You either break the silence, or it breaks you. So if you're holding something back right now, ask yourself: What am I actually protecting? And what is it costing me to keep protecting it?

Because silence isn't always safety. Sometimes, it's self-abandonment.

You're allowed to want peace. But peace doesn't come from avoiding the hard stuff. It comes from walking through it, with honesty, with heart, with boundaries, and with the kind of courage that doesn't wait for perfect timing. Don't suffer longer than necessary. If the conversation is already living in your head, bring it into the open. If it's stealing your sleep, your joy, your ease, it's time to let it out. You've survived worse than an awkward conversation. You can do this. And once you do?

You'll breathe again.

***

But...What about when it's *you* that you have to have the difficult conversation with? Let's talk about the difficult conversations with ourselves for a moment...

Not the ones where someone hurt you. The ones where you have to admit you've been the one crossing your own boundaries. The ones where you realize you were giving so much of yourself away that there was nothing left to stand on. I had one of those conversations yesterday. And it broke me. It wasn't because someone *took* too much.

It was because I gave too much.

I lost control of my time, not because it was stolen, but because I handed it over willingly. Piece by piece. I said yes because it brought me joy. Because I love helping. Because I *wanted* to be there. But love doesn't cancel out our capacity. Eventually, my mental health started cracking under the weight of it all. I kept trying to hold it together, thinking I could stretch myself just a little more. But joy turned into overwhelm. Passion turned into pressure. And what used to fill me up started draining me dry. So I had to make the call. I had to say the words. I had to let go of something I loved; and I hated every second of it.

That conversation wasn't even with someone else at first. It was with me. It was the moment I had to say, "This is too much." The moment I had to stop proving my strength and start protecting my peace. The moment I realized that choosing myself might look like quitting to others; but it was really a return. My reclamation.

But here's the part that really broke me open: It was my family paying the price. It was missing track meets and soccer games for my babies; while I was showing up and coaching someone else's. I was on the sidelines, cheering so loudly for other people's kids, and I meant every word of it. But mine were quietly noticing my absence. At first, they understood. They always do. They're kind and gracious and so deeply empathetic. But as the reschedules piled up; none of which were anyone's fault, I could feel the shift. It wasn't just one or two conflicts anymore. It was a slow, creeping loss of presence. And that's when I realized... I wasn't showing up fully for them because I wasn't even surviving fully for me.

I was buckling under the weight of my own expectations. Expectations that I had created. Expectations that said I had to keep going, keep doing, keep being strong. But I didn't feel strong. I felt scattered. I felt like I was giving everyone a version of me that was hanging on by a thread. And in that space... I felt like I was failing everywhere. So I made the hardest choice: To let go of something I loved...To say no to what I once said yes to... To reclaim what was never meant to be sacrificed in the first place. Not because I didn't care. But because I do. I owe it to my kids to show up as my best self. And lately... I haven't been.

I've been running ragged. Pushing past every signal my body gave me. Pouring out so much energy to hold everything together that by the time I got home, I had nothing left for the people who matter most. The laughter in our house went quiet. We lost our play. We lost our lightness. They started tiptoeing around me; not because they were afraid of me, but because they could feel I was on the edge of yet another breakdown. They didn't want to add weight to the pile I was already carrying. And that's what finally cracked me.

Because I never wanted to become the version of me who felt so brittle. So fragile. So unreachable. Last week, my body finally echoed what my spirit had been screaming. I found myself unwell; not just tired, but truly depleted. Another weekend left me completely drained, running on fumes, trying to push through like always. I was severely dehydrated, my body shutting down in quiet revolt, dangerously close to needing medical help. And my mental state? Crumbling. Everything felt loud. Everything felt heavy. Everything felt like too much.

And the thing that terrified me most wasn't the physical toll. It was the realization that I didn't even recognize myself anymore. The version of me who used to laugh loudly, who used to dance in the kitchen, who used to have energy for pillow fights and post-game chats and lingering bedtime stories; that version was buried under burnout. And that's when I knew I couldn't keep doing this. So I had the difficult conversation. The raw one. The honest one. The one I didn't want to have. Because I have the difficult conversations so I can find my peace. Even when it hurts. Even when it breaks my heart. Even when it feels like failure. Because sometimes, choosing peace doesn't feel peaceful at all, not at first. Peace isn't always soft. Sometimes it's brutal. Sometimes it's raw. Sometimes it's the only way back to yourself.

If you're in the middle of your own difficult conversation, whether with someone else or with yourself, I see you. You're not failing. You're recalibrating. You're allowed to choose you.

Reflection:

- What difficult conversation have I been avoiding?

- What truth have I been swallowing to keep the peace?

- What do I want from this conversation...clarity, closure, boundaries, reconnection?

- What am I afraid will happen if I speak up?

- What might *finally* happen if I do?

Conversation Costs vs. Conversation Gains
Why Saying the Hard Thing Is Worth It

The Cost of Avoiding the Conversation

The Gain of Having the Conversation

Sleepless nights and spiraling thoughts

Peace of mind, even if it's messy at first

Replaying scenarios in your head

Clarity, closure, or next steps

Physical tension in your body

A lighter, freer nervous system

Pretending things are fine when they're not

Authenticity and deeper self-trust

Resentment that builds silently

Respect, both for yourself and from others

Loss of connection

A more honest connection (even if fragile)

Self-doubt and internal blame

Self-trust and emotional relief

Burnout from over-giving or overthinking

Energy reclaimed, mentally, emotionally

Saying the hard thing is a breakthrough. But healing doesn't end when the words leave your mouth. It continues in the days that follow; when your actions either reinforce your truth or quietly undo it. Because there's a difference between speaking your peace and actually living in it.

It's one thing to say, "I deserve better." It's another to stop answering texts that make you feel small. It's one thing to say, "I love myself." It's another to look in the mirror and not flinch. It's one thing to set a boundary. It's another to honor it when it gets tested. That's where we go next.

You've done the talking. Now it's time for the showing.

CHAPTER NINE

SHOW AND TELL

There comes a moment in your healing where the mirror stops being enough. You've journaled. You've spoken the mantra. You've posted the quote. You've said the words. Healing doesn't just echo in your voice, it lands in your actions and eventually... your soul wants receipts. Because there's a difference between knowing the truth and living it. Let your actions speak the truth your words have been practicing.

You've talked about the boundaries. You've posted about letting go. You've cried in the car and whispered affirmations through clenched teeth. But now? Now comes the part no one can do for you. You have to **embody it.** You have to show what you've been trying to tell.

Because real healing doesn't just look like insight. It looks like action. It looks like alignment. It looks like tiny decisions behind-the-scenes that nobody claps for, but your soul notices.

Do you remember standing in front of the class during show-and-tell at school? Maybe you were excited, or nervous. Your hands were a little sweaty. Your voice maybe a little shaky. Holding up a toy you were SO excited to share. You didn't just talk about it. You showed it off proudly. You let people see something that mattered to you. You let yourself be seen! Healing asks for the same thing. But instead of a toy, it's your truth. Instead of a classroom, it's your life.

Let's be real. We've all been there, preaching peace, but still living in burnout. Posting the quote about self-love, then tearing ourselves apart in the mirror. Talking about boundaries but still texting back out of guilt. Saying we've let it go but still checking who watched our story. We mean well. We *want* to be that healed version of ourselves. But healing doesn't happen through performative spirituality or well-lit vulnerability. It happens when you stop *saying* the thing and start *embodying* it. It lives in the real, messy, un-Instagrammable moments where your actions finally catch up to your truth. If your body doesn't believe you, your nervous system doesn't either. It starts to trust you again when your choices stop contradicting your values.

Here's one of my favorite little gut-checks when something feels off:
Are my actions aligned with what I say I believe?

If not, there's a gap. And that gap will always feel like tension, confusion, or burnout. I say I want rest, but I keep proving I don't deserve it. I say I trust the process, but I keep micromanaging the outcome. I say I love myself, but I keep choosing people who don't. The *Alignment Gap* isn't about shame. It's about awareness. Let's close the gap. Not with pressure, but with *practice*.

Not perfectly either, just honestly.

Live a little truer. A little freer. A little more *you*.

***

Sometimes we're still not clear on it. Maybe what we label as anxiety or a funk, or hell, even the weird mood, is really just misalignment. You're saying one thing and doing another. You tell yourself you're worthy but keep burning out to prove it. You say you're protecting your energy, but still say yes when you want to say no. Your body can *feel* that gap and it gets tired of pretending. That weird ache in your chest? That frustration that shows up out of nowhere? That tension in your shoulders? That's you trying to live in misalignment. It's just because you're ready to start living in a way that actually reflects who you're becoming.

And when you do start showing your truth? It's terrifying. Because now it's witnessed. Now you're not just scribbling it in a journal, you're *living* it in public. That's where the fear comes in. "What if they think I'm too much?" "What if they see the old me come through again?" "What if I mess it up?" "What if I get it wrong?"

But here's what I've learned, people don't connect with your polished projection. They connect with your presence, your authenticity. They connect with the guts it takes to show up messy and to grow visibly. To live in your truth out loud, even when your voice shakes. You can practice confidence. You don't have to wait for it to arrive fully formed.

You can:

- Show up to the conversation you've been avoiding

- Ask for your needs instead of hoping someone reads your mind (I'm SUPER guilty of this one, but I'm working on being more forthcoming about my needs.)

- Wear the outfit even if your thighs touch and your arms aren't "toned"

- Share your story, even if your hands tremble

You're not here to *perform* confidence. This isn't about image. You're here to build trust with yourself. And you build it by showing up, again and again, even if it's not graceful. And that's where my work comes in, because I see it all the time in my studio. Women walk in scared, shaky and unsure. But underneath all of that?

Ready.

They're not just here for pretty pictures. They're here to reclaim something. To show up in front of the lens in ways they've never let themselves be seen. I've had clients cry before we even start. I've had women say, "I don't know what I'm doing here, I just know I need this." And every time, they walk out a little taller. Not because they became a different person. But because they remembered who they are. Boudoir is more than a photoshoot. It's the embodied truth.

It's witnessing yourself; fully, unapologeti-
cally, imperfectly...and deciding to stay. It was real bravery. Showing up scared
and doing it anyway.

It's the ritual now. Not the child version with a toy in your hand. The adult
version with your soul in your palm. "This is mine. This is what I've been
through. This is what I carry. This is what I love. This is what I believe." No
more hiding behind "I'm fine." No more polishing your pain to make it easier
for others to digest. No more saying the thing only when it's safe.

This is your truth. And you don't have to scream it. But you do have to **live** it.

Reflection:

- Where am I still performing instead of practicing?

- What truth have I been speaking, but not living?

- What's one small thing I could do this week to show the healing I've
  been telling myself I'm doing?

- If someone couldn't hear me speak, what would my actions say I
  believe about myself?

Healing isn't about being eloquent. It's about honesty. It's about matching your
energy to your values, even when it's quiet and when no one's watching. So, if
you've been showing up for everyone else? This is your moment to show up for
you.

Don't just say you're healing. Live it. Let your life become the story you don't
have to explain.

And here's the best part! Living your truth doesn't have to feel like labor.
It doesn't have to be another thing to get right, or another performance to
maintain. Because here's the secret most people miss: Embodiment gets easier
when you bring play into the process. When you stop trying to heal perfectly
and start dancing with it. When you let curiosity guide your next step instead
of pressure. When you allow your life to be less about proving, and more about
enjoying. You've said the thing. You're learning to live the thing. Now let's ask
a different question: *What if this could feel good, too?*

CHAPTER TEN

APPROACHING WORK WITH PLAYFULNESS

W e've been taught that work is supposed to be hard. That productivity is serious. That success only counts if you're exhausted by the end of it. Somewhere along the way, hustle became a badge of honor, and play became… immature. Lazy. Unproductive. Let's unlearn that. Because the more I heal, the more I realize something radical: Play isn't the opposite of work. It's the soul of it.

Play is a Frequency. Play is a vibration. It's energy. It's light. It's magnetic. When you enter a room with playfulness in your body, people feel it. They don't know why they're drawn to you, they just are. Because play is where creativity rests. It's where your voice comes alive. It's where your nervous system lets out a breath and says, "Yes…this. More of this."

Think about it.

Kindergarten used to be filled with building blocks and finger paint and wild little ideas that made no sense but sparked joy. Now? It's all structure. Rigor. Performance. Test scores. Even children have been taught to forget how to play. So it's no wonder that as adults, we're stuck in this endless loop of overwork,

shame, and striving. We've forgotten the very thing that makes creation feel alive.

My studio is my playground. Every year, I change up my entire boudoir studio. New sets. New lighting. New flow. Not because I need to. Not because it's broken. But because I *crave* it. Every time I reimagine the space, I remember that I'm allowed to evolve, too.

I crave the freedom to play, to explore, to create from a space of "What if?" People might think I'm wild for how often I shift things around. But I need that. My business is an extension of my energy, and my energy needs room to move. I want to play in the space I work in. That's how I make it feel like mine. That's how I keep it magnetic.

We've been sold the idea that joy is a reward. Something that comes *after* the work. After the checklist. After the body changes. After the inbox is clear. But what if joy is the fuel, not the finish line? You don't have to bleed to prove you're building something. What if letting yourself feel good now makes the workflow easier? Or makes the creativity bolder?  Makes you magnetic to the life you're building? What if joy isn't optional? What if it's the most honest measure of alignment you've got?

Let me be clear though, you can't force play. The minute you try to turn it into a productivity strategy, it dies. Really though. Forced play is where dreams go to die. It becomes just another task on the to-do list. Another thing to "get right."

That's not how play works. You don't force it. You *find* it. You follow the spark. You ask: What lights me up? What makes me lose track of time? What part of this feels fun, even if no one sees it? That's the doorway. Play is where your soul leads before your brain catches up.

What about when it gets too heavy? I know the feeling. You're stuck in the work. The obligations. The pressure. The pace. You're being so damn serious because "there's too much to do."

That's when I stop everything (now)... and I wrestle with my kids. Literally. I roughhouse with them. Or we play shut-the-box. Or video games. Sometimes we go to the park. We ride bikes. We play tag. Even my teenagers can't resist the pull of play. Because it's natural. It's embedded in us. We just buried it under all the "shoulds". When I start to spiral or get too heavy, I don't push through.

I shift. I play my way back to myself. What if I could challenge you to let it be fun?

Here's what I want you to ask:

- What if work could feel like a game?

- What if your goals could feel like experiments instead of pressure?

- What if creativity didn't have to be perfect to be powerful?

- What if the thing you're stuck on... isn't stuck at all?

- What if it's just waiting for you to loosen your grip?

Play isn't just for kids. It's not just for artists. It's not just for weekends or "free time." **Play is a life force.** And it's available to you right now.

You can play with:

- Your morning routine

- Your business strategy

- Your wardrobe

- Your calendar

- Your relationship

- Your food

- Your parenting

- Your healing

- Your spirituality

But Melissa, how do I play with those? Well, you stop asking, *"What's the right way?"* and start asking, *"What would feel fun today?"* You try the new coffee just because the label made you laugh. You set a timer and race the clock to finish the boring task. You wear the bold lipstick *just* to pick up groceries. You add a song to your morning routine that makes you dance while brushing your teeth. You send the risky text. You plan the date night. You wear the thing you think you can't pull off. You parent with a wink instead of a warning. You cook without measuring. You meditate to music. You doodle on your to-do list. You break the "rules" you didn't know you were still following.

Because play doesn't mean chaos, it means *aliveness*. It's how you shift out of autopilot and back into authorship. It's how you stop hiding from success and start *living* inside it. You don't wait for play to show up. You have to *invite* it in.

And no, it won't always feel natural at first. Especially if you've built a life on productivity, pressure, or people-pleasing. But play is a muscle. And every time you use it, it gets louder. Brighter. More contagious.

So if you're asking how...Start small. Start weird. Start *today*. Let it be light sometimes. Let it be messy. Let it be yours.

***

I paint. Not because I'm good at it. Trust me, I'm not. And not because I'm trying to become an artist. I'm also not. I paint because it lets me connect; with my kids, with my hands, with my nervous system. It's messy. It's unskilled. It's perfectly imperfect. We paint rocks. Canvases. Whatever's around. There are always half-finished pieces lying around our house, just beckoning someone to come play. And that's the point. It's not about being good at it, it's about being *in* it. Letting it be a form of meditation. Letting it be a release. Letting my kids see that I don't have to master something to love it.

Same with macramé. Same with scrapbooking (even if my third kid doesn't have one- sorry, buddy). I've let myself craft, fail, start over, abandon it, pick it up again. I let my hands do things. I let myself try. I let myself fail. Play isn't always loud or physical or full of laughter. Sometimes, it's just quietly losing yourself in the moment. Sometimes, it's choosing connection over outcome. And now? I even play with how I decorate my home. I stopped needing to Pinterest-perfect every corner. I stopped curating for strangers and started curating for joy.

My bathroom?

It's a hilarious little gallery wall filled with lions and other animals in tuxedos. They look so serious, so regal... and it cracks me up. Every. Single. Time. It's ridiculous. And it's mine. Honestly, that moment of laughter when I walk into that bathroom? That's a better ROI than any beige or grey trend could ever give me.

That's play. It doesn't have to match anything but your frequency. It doesn't have to be functional. It doesn't have to be praised. It just has to light you up.

Let your home smile back at you. Let your art be ugly. Let your creativity be wild and unhinged and completely unnecessary. That's where the magic lives.

Here's some helpful reflections:

- Where have I made work too serious?

- What would it look like to bring more play into my process?

- What did I love to do as a kid that I've abandoned?

- What if I didn't need to "earn" rest, joy, or laughter?

- Where am I using "I'll be happy when..." logic in my life or work?

- What would change if I brought joy into the process instead of waiting for the outcome?

You don't have to hustle your way into alignment. You can play your way into it. You don't have to prove you're worthy of joy. You just have to stop resisting it. Let your work feel good. Let your ideas be weird. Let your business be fun again. You are allowed to create from curiosity instead of pressure. You are allowed to enjoy the process. You are allowed to laugh, even while you're healing. Play isn't a luxury. It's a portal. Step through it.

The more you play, the more your soul comes alive. But sometimes, the moment you loosen your grip... a voice tightens it again. The one that tells you it's "too much." Too loud. Too messy. Too selfish. Too unserious. That's the voice we need to meet next.

Because healing isn't just about learning to enjoy life again, it's about learning to do it without permission. Let's talk about the part of you that still thinks joy is a problem.

Let's talk about her.

CHAPTER ELEVEN

REMOVING THE JUDGEY ADULT

Let's clear something up real quick before we even get into this, because this one confuses a lot of people on the healing path. **Ego and the Judgey Adult aren't the same.** They're partners in crime. They are cousins. Same fear, different tactics.

Both of them exist to keep you safe... but their version of "safe" is small. Controlled. Predictable. **Ego** is internal. She's the voice inside your head that second-guesses everything. She whispers doubt, pumps the brakes, hands you excuses that sound like care. She's sneaky. She plays defense. She doesn't want you embarrassed, exposed, or disappointed. So, she talks you out of things before you even try.

But **the Judgey Adult**? She's external. Her job isn't to protect your feelings, it's to protect your image. She wants you polished, presentable, and palatable. She's the "what will people think?" voice. The one who's scanning the room, adjusting your tone, fixing your posture. She doesn't stop you from showing up, she just tries to sanitize it.

Where Ego says:

"You're not ready."
"What if you fail?"
"Let's wait until it's perfect."

79

The Judgey Adult says:

"That's not appropriate."
"You're being dramatic."
"That's not how grown-ups behave."

Ego fears failure. The Judgey Adult fears judgment.
One keeps you hidden. The other lets you be seen, but only if you're edited.

They're two sides of the same survival coin, both trying to keep you in check. Not because they're evil, but because at some point, someone taught you that being your full, messy, emotional, expressive self wasn't safe.

So, when you do start to heal? When you let joy in, speak up, rest without guilt, or post that bold-ass photo of yourself? Ego tries to pull you back into the shadows and the Judgey Adult tries to cover you in beige.

And neither of them gets the final say now.

Joy is rebellion when you were raised to perform. Rest is resistance when you were taught to hustle. Play is power when you were told to behave.

You've invited joy back in. You've let yourself play. You've loosened your grip. You finally let yourself enjoy the moment. But then...BAM. She shows up. The inner adult with the crossed arms and permanent scowl. The one who scolds you for dreaming big, resting too long, doing things "wrong," or god forbid... enjoying yourself. She's the one who whispers:
"That's not responsible."
"That's embarrassing."
"You look ridiculous."
"You should know better."

She doesn't throw tantrums, she throws shade. She doesn't yell, she judges. She doesn't argue, she shames. She's not loud, she's passive-aggressive as hell. But she is *always* there, like a pop-up notification for guilt and self-doubt.

Mine? She's everything I was taught to become. Put-together. Measured. Constantly on alert. She's poised and polished, like an old boss with an outdated handbook. And she's exhausted. Because all she does is monitor and manage, criticize and correct. She thinks she's protecting me, keeping things "safe". But what she's really doing is choking the joy out of everything.

I started noticing her the moment I decided not to live a "normal" life. When I said no the "rules", like the traditional 9-5. When I carved my own path. When I leaned into creativity instead of conformity. When I dared to be loud, visible, and unapologetic about what I wanted. She showed up panicked with a clipboard full of warnings:
"That's not realistic."
"You don't have a backup plan."
"People are going to talk."
"This is reckless."

At first, I bought it. I thought she was wise. Responsible even. But let's be honest, like Ego, she's not mature, she's afraid. Her voice wasn't rooted in truth. It was rooted in everything I was taught to be afraid of.

She sounds like authority figures you once trusted. Like the teacher who told you that you were "too much." Like the family member who said you were "just being dramatic". Or like the coworker who rolled their eyes at your dream and the boss who wanted you to stay small and silent.

She sounds like the voices you loved most, but weaponized by fear, then internalized by you. Any of these sound familiar?

"You should know better."
"You can't do it like that."
"People like you don't get to..."
"You're too much."
"You're not enough."

These are all things I've personally dealt with. I'm giving you as many examples as I can, because she's sneaky and you may not realize what her voice sounds like. Oh! And she thrives when you're growing. Because growth is unknown. And like Ego, the unknown terrifies her. So we have to become aware so we can stop her in her tracks.

There was a day, not that long ago, when the Judgey Adult nearly won. I had just refreshed my studio. I was so excited; the new textures, new props, a slightly unhinged chandelier I was weirdly obsessed with. The space felt alive. *I* felt alive. And then I opened my inbox. Someone had replied to a behind-the-scenes video I posted on Instagram: "This feels really unprofessional. Why not just stick to clean, classic setups?"

Once again, there she was. My inner adult practically leapt to her feet. "See? This is what happens when you lean into what you like. Why do you have to stand out? Why can't you just be normal?" I spiraled. I started second-guessing everything. Maybe the space *was* too much. Maybe I should've gone more polished. Maybe I was being "too creative."

But then I caught myself, **What am I fighting for?**

I'm not building a business for the beige crowd. I'm not creating for critics who want quiet conformity. I'm building something *real. Energetic. Honest. Mine.* I'm not for everyone. And that's the point. So I shut my laptop. I walked into my studio. I took a slow, deep breath. And I let myself feel proud. Because despite the judgment, internal and external, this space felt like *me*. And that matters more than one stranger's opinion in my inbox. That's what I'm fighting for.

Want to know what sets the Judgey Adult off the most? **Joy.** Because joy is chaos to her. It isn't measurable. It's not scheduled. It doesn't come with a five-step plan or a sense of control. Joy is unpredictable. It doesn't fit into her spreadsheet of acceptable behavior. So every time I...

- Play with my kids instead of folding laundry

- Paint badly

- Dance in the kitchen

- Laugh too loudly in public

- Decorate my bathroom with lions in tuxedos

- Rest without "earning" it

- Spend money on something that made me feel alive instead of something "practical"

...she *loses her mind*. But *me*? I come back to life.

Here's the thing though. You don't need her permission or approval. One of the most toxic beliefs we carry is that joy, rest, and expression must be earned. That you have to be "caught up" to relax. That you have to prove yourself to be allowed to play. That you have to shrink yourself to be loved. It's a lie. The judgey adult is constantly trying to make you palatable. She's trying to keep you predictable. But guess what? Your magic isn't in your predictability. It's in your expansion. You do not need her permission to grow. You do not need her permission to laugh. You do not need her permission to do it differently.

So, am I fighting to feel proud of the life I'm creating?
Am I fighting to live in alignment with what matters to me?
Am I fighting to raise kids who see joy as normal, not earned?
Am I fighting to break cycles that kept generations silent and scared? Because every time I answer that question honestly, her voice gets smaller.

She'll always have opinions. But I'm not living my life for her anymore.

Because every time I answer that question honestly, her voice gets smaller. She may still talk. But I'm no longer listening. Honestly, when she talks now, I almost use that as a confirmation that I'm on the right path. And here's the thing, she's not evil. She's just scared. She was created by systems, by survival, by stories that were never yours to begin with. She thinks she's keeping you safe. She doesn't realize she's just keeping you stuck. I grew up hearing things like, "Jobs are jobs, you just have to deal with it." "Ya, you might be miserable...that's what weekends are for." That mindset buries its way in deep. It teaches you to tolerate a life that doesn't light you up...because lighting up feels selfish. Or unrealistic. Or worse... irresponsible. So when I started chasing something that actually *felt* good? That old programming kicked in hard. The Judgey Adult called it reckless. But it wasn't reckless. It was alignment.

So let her talk. Then thank her for her concern and show her the damn door.

"I'm not that little girl anymore. I can hold my own now."

Reflection

Time to get real.

- What does your inner Judgey Adult say the most?

- Whose voice does it sound like?

- What's something you've wanted to do, but haven't because you were afraid of being judged?

Now flip it:

- **What are you fighting for?**

- What do you *gain* if you do it anyway?

- What do you *lose* if you keep shrinking to keep her comfortable?

Write it. Say it. Then *go do the damn thing*. Because here's the truth:

She's always going to have something to say. Let her say her piece. Then go laugh anyway. Go create the weird thing. Go rest in the middle of the mess. Go take up space before you feel "ready." You don't have to become the polished, filtered, beige version of yourself to be lovable or successful or wise. You just have to become the *real* one. And the real you? She's got paint on her hands. Music playing loud. A messy room. A belly laugh. And *no apologies*.

That's the version you're fighting for.

The Judgey Adult doesn't just police your joy... she's also obsessed with measuring your worth. And one of her favorite yardsticks? Money. She'll tell you you're only valuable if you're producing. Only worthy if you're earning. Only "doing it right" if you've got something to show for it. But that's not truth. That's a lie dressed up like strategy. So, let's break into that next.

CHAPTER TWELVE

DON'T PUT MONEY ON A PEDESTAL

*M*oney is not your worth. It's not your proof. It's just a tool. And when you stop worshipping it, you stop betraying yourself to earn it.

For a long time, I chased money like it held the keys to everything I wanted. Success. Stability. Validation. Safety. I saw money as proof that I was doing something right. If I had it...I was enough. If I didn't...I was failing.

I didn't just want money, I craved it like a drug. I needed it to prove I was worth something. That I wasn't failing or falling behind. But what I've come to learn (and it's been a process) is that money is just a tool. Not a ruler. Not a mirror. Not a measure of worth.

Just a tool.

I used to think *more* money would make me feel safe. Like if I could just hit the next milestone, the next revenue goal, the next paycheck... then I could finally breathe. But the more I chased, the emptier it felt. Because chasing money doesn't fill you up, it keeps you running. It makes you perform. It makes you shape-shift. It makes you say yes when your body's screaming no. You begin building a life around numbers instead of values. And one day you look around and realize... none of it even feels like you. It's not just burnout. Now it's disconnection in a fancy outfit.

Ironically, the point in our lives when we had the most money (by our standards) was also the point I felt the most depleted. Okay but, don't get it twisted, "the most money" for us was still under $14,000 in the bank. A number that might feel laughable to some. But when you're used to living month to month, that number felt massive. We were finally "doing it." We were hitting goals. We were seeing green.

But I was burning out. No time to rest. No time to play. No time to actually enjoy the life we were building. I was exhausted, constantly overbooked, and spiritually flatlined.

That's when Koko and I found the phrase:

Suffering your success.

And it stuck. We say it often now, as a kind of gut-check: "Are we suffering our success?" Because what's the point of financial success if it costs you everything else?

And now... Right now? We're back at a low point. Painfully low. The kind of low where you check your account before pumping gas. The kind of low where you're doing financial gymnastics just to make it through the week. Where shame rides shotgun and every swipe of the debit card feels like a risk. Where your brain wants to spiral, your chest stays tight, and every decision feels loaded with fear.

And yet? I swear, it's the book writing itself. I *have* to be _here_ again to *feel* it. To write this part authentically. To know what it's like to sit in the gap, between fear and faith. Between bills and belief. Between scarcity and self-trust. Because this is the part no one glamorizes. Desperation is painful. Desperation is *repellent*. You cannot attract abundance while the cloud of "please just let this work" hangs heavy over every decision. So how do we shift out of it? We don't fake positivity. We choose assurance. "Money always flows to me." "I'm held." "This is temporary, not permanent." "I don't have to perform to be supported."

This is the work. This is the stretch. This is the medicine I wouldn't wish on anyone; except I know how powerful it is once it alchemizes. Even now, as I'm editing this book, we've once again fallen on hard times. Not because we were careless, but because we were leading with heart. We paid for the kids' braces in full. Covered upcoming trips in full. We poured into what mattered: our children, their growth, their experiences. And then came back-to-back out-of-town soccer tournaments, 8th grade graduations, moving-up ceremonies, specialty cameras for soccer, braces, glasses, car problems, more expenses, more travel. Our account got hit again and again, until it was barely hanging on.

After graduation, our tradition has always been to celebrate. To eat together. To take a moment and mark the milestone with joy. And even though the numbers in the account were grim, I looked at Koko and said, "We lead with values. We're still going out to eat."

So we did. We laughed, we took pictures, we made a memory.

And two days later? We were gathering cash from around the house to deposit and keep the account from going negative. But I don't regret it. Because money will come and go. It always has. But these fleeting moments with the people we love? Those are the ones we're building our life around. That's the wealth I'm after.

I don't want the bank account to look good while our joy dries up. I want to make it to every track meet. Help buy our oldest his first car. Surprise him with a new set of golf clubs because he's finally finding his rhythm. I want to say yes to our daughter's travel soccer trips, ID camps, and extra training sessions, not because it makes sense on paper, but because she lights up every time she plays.

I want to fund private sessions for our youngest, coach his team, cheer from the sidelines, and be part of this phase where he still wants me there for all of it. We don't want money to dictate what matters. We want to lead with our values, and let the money rise up to support that.

And weirdly? The more we do that, the more abundance shows up. Not just in our bank account, but in our days. Our joy. Our freedom.

There was a time I underpriced a full-day shoot just to land the gig, because I was scared to lose it. I knew it wasn't aligned. I felt it in my gut. But I smiled. Took the job. Pushed through. And when it was over? I wasn't proud. I wasn't fulfilled. I didn't even feel "safe", the money wasn't enough to fix the feeling that

I had sold myself short. That's the thing about betraying your worth: it always leaves a bruise.

Money was always a thing in my family. Not in a flashy, luxurious way, but in a "we work hard, we earn what we get" kind of way. It was serious. It was survival. It was sacred. And because of that, I absorbed a belief early on:
Money = Success = Worth

If you had it, you were doing something right. If you didn't, something was wrong with you. So even as I started building my own version of success, I kept dragging those beliefs with me. And every time I had a slow month or a dip in income?

I questioned me. Not the system. Not the season. **Me.**

I felt worthless. Like the number in my bank account was a reflection of my value. Like if I wasn't producing, I wasn't enough. That's how deep the story ran.

Here's what I believe now: **Money is energy.** It flows. It responds. It amplifies. It moves.

Money can support you, but it cannot save you. Money can create comfort, but it cannot create peace. Money can fund your dreams, but it cannot give you purpose. It's just a tool. And if you place it on a pedestal, you'll start betraying yourself just to reach it. This is my new anchor. **I let values drive my decisions, not money.** Does that mean I don't care about money? Of course not.

But I'm not letting it decide how I show up, or who I become, or what I say yes or no to. Money might talk, but my values drive. And I'm not handing my bank account the damn wheel. I want to look back and know I stayed true. That I didn't sell out my alignment for a short-term gain. That I created from a place of integrity, not desperation.

And here's the beautiful paradox: When I stopped pedestalizing money, I actually started attracting more of it. Because it wasn't in charge of me anymore.

Side note:

And one more thing I've come to believe deep in my bones...The Universe is *always* listening. *Always* responding. And its answer is almost always: *yes*. Not yes like approval.

Yes like echo. It agrees with you.

If you say, "I'm broke," the Universe doesn't argue. It just gently says, "Yes. Let's keep reinforcing that." If you say, "I'm barely hanging on," It meets you there with more reasons to feel stretched thin. If you say, "I hope we make it..." The Universe responds, "Yes. Keep hoping."

It's not cruel. It's not punishing you. It's just aligning with what you're energetically rehearsing. The Universe believes you. That's the part that shook me.

It **_believes_** you.

So you have to start being more intentional about what you're teaching it to believe. This is why I don't affirm from a place of perfection. I affirm from a place of re-direction. Even when it feels like we're on our last dollar, I try not to say, "We're screwed." Instead, I whisper, "We've been here before and we made it through. We always do." Instead of "There's never enough," I try to say, "Everything I need is already on its way." And instead of "I'm desperate," I reach for "I'm supported. I'm held. I'm making aligned moves, even when it's hard."

Because the Universe is always tuned in. And when I speak from desperation, I get more reasons to panic. But when I speak from assurance (even while trembling) I start to notice the openings again. The little moments of relief. The nudges. The signs.

And it's not about being fake or bypassing what's hard. It's about anchoring into something truer than the fear. Fear feels real. But so does faith. And I get to decide which one I'm amplifying. Because at the end of the day, I don't want to rehearse lack and then be surprised when scarcity shows up. I want to start rehearsing peace. Provision. Overflow. Even before it makes sense on paper. So when I say, "Money flows to me," I'm not just saying pretty words. I'm speaking into alignment.

I'm reminding the Universe what to say yes to.

It believes you.

Reflection: Let's Check Your Alignment

- What story were you told about money growing up?

- When have you compromised your values in pursuit of money?

- When have you chosen alignment over income, and how did it feel?

- What does true success look like for you, outside of numbers?

Finish the sentence:
I don't want to suffer my success. I want to_____.
I don't want the money to feel like power. I want it to feel like
_____.

Reframing:
Money is a tool, not a trophy.
Money is a partner, not a parent.
Money is a resource, not a ruler.
Money doesn't get to grade your worth.

You're allowed to be wealthy. You're allowed to thrive. You're allowed to want
more. But you don't have to betray yourself
to get there. When you lead with values,
money becomes the side effect, not the finish line.

CHAPTER THIRTEEN

HAPPY MONEY

M oney carries the energy you give it. Spend in fear, and it shrinks. Spend in gratitude, and it grows. So much of our suffering around money comes from what we believe it means about us. How much we have. How much we don't. What we earn. What we owe. But once you stop pedestalizing money, and once you stop giving it the power to define your worth, you get to ask a different question:

What kind of energy do I want my money to carry?

Because money doesn't just fund your life. It *reflects* it. Let's talk about how that energy changes when money starts to feel safe. When it feels intentional. Grateful. Alive.

Let's talk about Happy Money.

Real talk. We used to pay bills with frustration. The number in our account would drop to almost nothing, and we'd sit there trying to figure out which bill could wait. Rent? No. Electric? Not if we wanted the A/C to stay on. Internet? God forbid the kids lose their connection to school. And every time, Koko would say: "We'll have enough. Something will come through. It always does."

Which—let me tell you—is the most annoying thing to hear when you're staring at an empty account. And in some ways, the most comforting. Because he was always right.

But here's what we didn't realize back then: We weren't just paying bills. We were pouring out desperate money. **Survival energy. Scramble energy.** We weren't investing. We were hustling out of fear, swiping cards with our teeth clenched, praying the payment would clear. That's not a life...that's a slow suffocation. Every payment felt like a threat. Every transaction, a reminder of how close we were to not making it. And the Universe? It matched us right back. We were always putting out the hope: "I hope we have enough to make bills." And so the Universe always delivered... just enough to make bills. Sometimes late. Sometimes barely. Sometimes with a few bucks left over. But never more. Never ease. Never overflow.

Because we hadn't asked for more. We weren't living like more was available to us. We weren't ready to receive it, because we didn't believe we were allowed to.

From Just Enough to More Than Enough

Everything changed the moment we had our shakeup. The house we'd rented for ten years was being sold while the market was high. We had two months to get out. Our lives got flipped upside down. And the Universe said: *Comfort isn't going to cut it anymore.*

We moved. We recalibrated. We rethought everything. And slowly, something shifted. I started charging my worth (which, let's be honest, is a whole other book). We started building something aligned. We stopped surviving and started choosing. We stopped asking, "Can we afford it?" And started asking, "Is this aligned?" It wasn't about being reckless. It was about deciding we were worth more than just scraping by.

The Universe noticed.

That $150 cushion in our bank account became $1,000. Then a little more. Then more still. Now, every time I find a penny on the ground, I say: "Thanks, Universe. More please." And the wild part? I find more. Not because I'm chasing. But because I'm open. Because I trust. Because I celebrate the little things like they're the big things.

Happy Money is more than just a mindset. It's an energetic pattern. Desperate money leaves you depleted. Angry money feels like a punishment. Fear-based money creates lack. Shame money makes you small.

But Happy Money?

It moves freely. It celebrates you. It reflects trust. It multiplies in ways you can't predict. The other day I bought my favorite overpriced coffee just because it reminded me, I'm alive. I took a sip, closed my eyes, and whispered "thank you" ...not to the coffee, but to the moment. That's Happy Money. The moment you stop spending with resentment and start spending with intention, everything changes. We used to feel dread when bills hit. Now? We're working on feeling gratitude. Sure, it's not always fun to pay bills. But look at what those bills represent: A roof over your head. Internet that lets your kids access the world. Lights that stay on during your late-night breakthroughs. Heat or A/C so your family is safe and cozy. Bills are a tax on the life you've built. If you're unhappy with those bills, then that's the signal to reset your life, not your gratitude.

We Talk About Money with Our Kids

Unpopular opinion? Maybe. But we include our kids in money conversations. Not every gritty detail. Not adult-level panic. But we do talk about it, openly, lovingly, and honestly.

Why? Because shame thrives in silence. And if there's one thing we're trying to break in this family, it's the idea that money struggles equal failure.

We talk about why we can't afford something right now. Not to burden them, but to show them that budgeting isn't punishment, it's management. It's being mindful. It's prioritizing. It's choosing long-term peace over short-term approval.

We explain that the usual "yes" might turn into a "not this time" because we're working toward something bigger. Because bills don't disappear. Because we want to stay in alignment with what matters most...and sometimes that means making hard decisions.

And we talk about emotions, too. Why Mom or Dad might be a little more on edge. Why there's tension in the room. Not to make them feel responsible, but to model transparency over repression.

Because kids *feel* it anyway. The mood shifts. The sighs. The way we scroll through numbers at the kitchen table.

So instead of leaving them to wonder or internalize it, we name it.

We say,
"This isn't about you."
"We're in a tight spot right now, and it's stressful."
"We're figuring it out, and we'll get through it together."

When we shared how we used to feel ashamed of money struggles, we saw their faces soften. We saw how deeply they *listened*. How *seen* they felt. Because truth-telling creates safety. And our kids deserve that kind of safety...the kind that says, struggling doesn't make you a failure. Silence doesn't make you strong. Pretending doesn't make it go away. And maybe most of all: You're still allowed to dream big... even if your parents are tightening the grocery budget.

This is how we break the cycle. No more shame. No more silence. Just weathering together.

***

Now sometimes, happy money looks like spending on something that seems a little reckless but is *deeply* recharging. Maybe it's a last-minute trip. Or a random dinner out. Maybe it's the overpriced but joy-giving thing. I'm not saying go wild. But when the opportunity to invest in your joy presents itself, **consider it sacred**. That's Happy Money. Because joy creates momentum. And when you're vibrating high, you know, full of gratitude, lightness, and aliveness - that's the energy that returns to you.

But let's be real. It's hard to feel empowered around money when you're barely making it. I've been there. (Shit, as I'm editing this book-I'm here now!) We've sat at the gas pump deciding how many dollars we could spend. We've stretched groceries. We've cried over overdraft fees. This isn't about toxic positivity. This is about **hopeful honesty**. It's about saying: *"This isn't where I want to stay...*

but it's not where I'll end." Because the energy you bring to your current finances creates the foundation for what's coming next.

Talk to your money like it matters. Even if it's not much. **Especially** when it's not much. Bless every dollar. Thank it for showing up. Tell it what you'd like it to do next. Money loves having a job. It loves having a purpose. Let it be with love.

***

Mantra Box: Spend With Intention

Try these as mantras when spending, saving, or even stressing about money:

- "Thanks, Universe. More please."

- "Every dollar I spend returns to me doubled."

- "Money flows to me easily and often."

- "I spend with trust. I receive with joy."

- "Money supports the life I'm building."

- "This payment is a blessing for the comfort it brings."

- "There's always more where that came from."

- "I am grateful for what money makes possible."

- "My money reflects my values."

- "Spending is a sacred exchange."

Use these especially when you feel old patterns creeping in.

Reflection:

How do you feel before, during, and after spending money?

Do you tense up at checkout?

Do you feel guilt after purchases, even necessary ones?

Can you spot the difference between anxious spending and intentional investing?

Now I challenge you to journal this:

What is my current relationship with money trying to teach me? Where am I spending from fear instead of flow? How would it feel to spend money with gratitude, no matter the amount?

Don't judge your answers. Just witness them.

Practice: Reframe Your Spending

OLD THOUGHT

HAPPY MONEY REFRAME

ugh, another bill

This bill is proof of the life I've built

I can't believe groceries cost this much.

I'm grateful we're fed and nourished.

This wipes out my account.

> This supports joy, and more is on the way.

> I hate spending money on this.

> This is helping me stay warm / safe / supported.

> I shouldn't have bought that.

> That purchase brought lightness…and that matters.

Start small. One reframe at a time. Let it become your default.

Happy Money isn't about how much you have. It's about how you relate to it. It's money that moves with gratitude. Money that aligns with your values. Money that honors the life you're building, not the one you're trying to keep up with. So next time you feel the shame creep in…The fear. The scarcity. The guilt…Ask yourself:

What would it look like to let money be happy in my hands?

And then…start there. Because money is energy, and so is joy. And if Happy Money taught me anything, it's that how we spend our energy matters just as much as how we spend our dollars. So when the bills are paid, when the survival scramble slows down, when the space to breathe opens up again… You get to ask:

What do I want this life to sound like?
Not just what it costs. Not just what it produces. But what it *feels* like in the room when no one's watching. And for me? When survival softens into stability, and joy begins to echo again, I hear it. Not just in dollars… in rhythm. In laughter at the dinner table. In the soundtrack of a life we're finally living, not just surviving.

That always comes back to music.

CHAPTER FOURTEEN

LAUGH, PLAY MUSIC, MAKE A SOUNDTRACK TO YOUR LIFE

I f you're wondering why everything feels flat lately, ask yourself this: When was the last time you felt joy on purpose, not just by accident? If your life had a soundtrack, would it be silence? Or would it sing your joy back to you?

Think about it. Every movie, TV show, even your favorite TikTok's have a score. There's a soundtrack playing underneath everything. And if you're anything like me... that soundtrack is essential. I can't function without music playing. It's the heartbeat of our home. The vibe of our garage. The mood for my sessions. The energy that fills the gaps when words just don't cut it.

We use Amazon Music and create playlist after playlist. We can literally look back and see the eras of our lives through the names of those playlists. The heartbreak years. The healing years. The hustle seasons. The soft landings. Funny enough, we realized something one day that hit way too hard:

Our darkest days? The hardest seasons? They had no soundtrack. We weren't playing music at all. And that silence reflected exactly how we were feeling.

Music shifts the energy in the room before anyone opens their mouth. It lifts the fog. It gets you out of your head and into your body. It helps you exhale when you didn't even realize you were holding your breath. I've started to believe music is its own form of prayer. A vibration your soul recognizes before your mind does. It's how I shift the energy. It's how I protect my peace. It's how I call myself back when I start to drift.

Sometimes I don't even know what I'm feeling until a song pulls it up and out of me. I've found clarity in a beat drop. I've processed frustration in a bridge. I've felt understood in a lyric that sounds like it was written just for me. Music isn't background, it's guidance. It's a portal. It's how I remember who the hell I am.

I remember one night; I was deep in a spiral. Life felt heavy. I felt behind. Everything felt too loud and too quiet at the same time. I was sitting in the garage, just... numb. And then Koko hit play.

"Light My Love" by Greta Van Fleet.

The second that guitar hit, I felt it. Something in me stirred. It was like the song dropped a rope down into my chest and gently pulled me back to myself. Not fixed. Not fully better. But present. And sometimes, that's enough. We didn't even talk about it. We just sat there, letting it play.

That's what music does. It moves the pieces that words can't reach.

Mason (my oldest) found my "Melissa" playlist once. It was all the stuff I loved in my teens: My Chemical Romance, Red Jumpsuit Apparatus, Taking Back Sunday, Fall Out Boy, Bullet for My Valentine, Coheed and Cambria, Blink 182... Watching him fall into my old genre was the coolest full-circle moment. We connected through power chords and screaming choruses. We'd blast it in the car and laugh so hard at the lyrics, but also somehow feel them, like we were both angsty, emotional teens at the same time. (Which, honestly, we kind of were.) Music gives us portals to meet each other across generations. It gives our kids access to who we were before we became parents. Before the responsibilities. Before the exhaustion. Before all the "shoulds."

Those drives with him? That was our soundtrack. The volume loud. Speakers maxed out. A connection that didn't need to be explained, just felt.

Now, my daughter has stumbled across that same playlist. And once again, I get to relive that season, but differently. She connects to different songs than he did. She plays them loud. She sings them soft. She uses them to feel big emotions I didn't even know she had yet. And I get to witness her becoming. Through the same music that helped me do the same.

That same scream-singing, moody, nostalgic playlist became the backdrop to some of my favorite moments during the pandemic lockdown. Two of my girlfriends and I would drag our soccer chairs out to the edge of a cul-de-sac that dead-ended into the desert. We'd sit far apart, wrapped in blankets, a Bluetooth speaker in the center like our own little sacred campfire. We'd play the playlist on repeat, not because we were stuck in the past, but because we needed something familiar. Something real. Something that didn't require effort to feel good.

We'd unwrap our fears, talk about parenting in a pandemic, laugh until we couldn't breathe, and sit in the kind of silence that only happens when you're completely safe. That playlist made us feel like teenagers again. Like life wasn't crumbling. Like there was still joy and rebellion and something to hold on to. It wasn't just music. It was an anchor. A retreat. A sacred thread that wove us together while everything else felt like it was falling apart.

Koko and I create new playlists every so often... but this is the one that's playing on loop right now. We call it **Home Glow**, because that's exactly what it feels like: warm, honest, familiar. A mix of soul, depth, movement, and vibe. This is the soundtrack to our real life; our garage talks, chaotic dinners, post-session resets, and the "bring me back to myself" vibe.

Some of the songs that are holding us right now:

"I Think I Like When It Rains" – WILLIS
"Dark Red" – Steve Lacy"
From Eden" – Hozier
"Lose Control" – Teddy Swims
"Beyond" – Leon Bridges
"Someone New" – Hozier
"Wondering Why" – The Red Clay Strays
"Rain" – The Teskey Brothers
"Pour Me Out" – Kashus Culpepper
"Ends of the Earth" – Ty Myers
"Colors" – Black Pumas

"Pain and Misery" – The Teskey Brothers
"Love The Hell Out of You" – Lewis Capaldi
"ALL MY LOVE" – Coldplay
"Light My Love" – Greta Van Fleet
"I'm Still Fine" – The Red Clay Strays

Some of these songs ground us. Some lift the weight. Some remind us how soft it's okay to be. And some just vibe so hard you can't help but feel alive again.

Music doesn't just live in your ears. It lives in your body. If you've forgotten what joy feels like... move to music. Dance in your kitchen. Sway in your chair. Stretch on the floor while a song plays like it was made just for this moment. Let yourself feel silly. Let yourself be awkward. Let yourself enjoy something you don't have to earn. This isn't about performing. It's about *accessing* a frequency you were born to carry. If you're waiting to feel 'ready' before you dance, let me save you the suspense...you won't. Not until you move anyway. Not until you shake the stuck-ness out of your bones and stop asking your mind for permission your soul already gave you.

Reflection: Build Your Soundtrack

Create your life's playlist in real time. Use these questions to get started:

- What song makes you feel powerful? Like walk-through-fire, no-one-can-stop-me energy?

- What song makes you feel soft? Safe? Nostalgic?

- What's a song that instantly makes you laugh or move your body?

- What was the soundtrack to one of the hardest seasons of your life?

- What's a song that helped you heal, even if you didn't realize it at the time?

Now open your music app and create a playlist that speaks to your soul right now. Don't curate it to sound impressive. Curate it to feel true. Let it hold the chaos and the joy. The quiet and the rage. The expansion and the in-between. Let it be the music you didn't know you needed, until now.

You've done so much healing work. You've faced the shadows. You've questioned the stories. You've learned to listen inward. Now let this be the part where you let joy in. Where you turn the volume up. Where you laugh from your belly and sing terribly in the car and dance in your kitchen like no one's watching, because honestly, they aren't. And even if they are... who cares? Healing without joy isn't healing. Don't forget, you're not just here to fix yourself. You're here to *feel* yourself. Loudly, shamelessly, and fully.

Let this chapter be your permission slip to feel good. To create moments that feel like you again. To be messy. To be loud. To be alive. You've earned that. Not when you heal everything. Not when it's all fixed. But now. In the middle of the chaos.

Right here.

Right now.

Stop waiting for the chaos to calm down before you live your life. This *is* your life. The joy doesn't come *after* the storm, it's what keeps you from drowning in it.

Press play.

Music reminds us to feel. To move with the rhythm of the moment instead of getting stuck in the weight of overthinking. Because here's the thing: Life isn't a perfectly scored film where everything lines up with the beat. Sometimes the notes are messy. Sometimes they're off-key. Sometimes you choose the wrong playlist (or the wrong path). But you keep listening. You adjust the volume. You press play again. And that's what decisions are like. Not perfect. Just present. Just yours. So as we turn the page, I want to talk about the pressure to choose "right", and how freeing it is when you realize you don't have to.

You just have to keep showing up to the life you're creating. One beat at a time. And when in doubt? Turn it up. Feel it loud. Let the music remind you, you're still here. Still healing. Still dancing. Still yours.

Chapter Fifteen

There's No Perfect Decision

You don't need the perfect answer. You need a little courage, a little clarity, and the guts to build something honest from wherever the hell you are.

Life doesn't have a script. It has a soundtrack. And sometimes, what we need more than the "right" answer... is rhythm. Presence. The courage to choose what feels aligned, even if it's not guaranteed.

We live in a world that loves the idea of the *right* choice. The one golden answer that will unlock the future we want. The path that leads to success, fulfillment, security. The decision that proves we did everything right. But here's the truth no one tells you:

There is no perfect decision.

There's just the one you make and the life you build around it. Every decision comes with a cost. Every option has a shadow side. Every yes means saying no to something else. And no matter how long you agonize, no matter how many lists you make, you won't know how it all plays out until you live it.

So, let's get this out of the way: You're going to wonder *what if.* (Of fucking course you are) You're going to grieve roads not taken. You're going to think back and try to reverse-engineer your path like a detective looking for where things went "wrong." But hear me on this: You did not make a wrong choice.

You made the best choice you could with what you knew at the time. And that's all we can ever do.

Recently, my daughter had to choose which high school to attend, one known for academics and being the newest school in town, the other known for athletics and a tight-knit friend group she loved. And it wasn't easy. There was no clear winner, just two doors that each led to a different version of her life. She agonized. We talked. We weighed every pro and con. And even now, after she made her decision, there are still moments she wonders if she chose right.

And that's okay. Because what we reminded her (what we keep reminding ourselves) is that once you choose, *that's the path*. You can't live in the alternate version forever. You build the life you want on the road you're walking now.

My oldest son faced something similar when he had to choose between continuing golf, something he was good at and had committed to, or pursuing track, which had started calling to him in a new way. There wasn't a wrong answer, but there wasn't a perfect one either. And like his sister, he wrestled with that. There were pros and cons either way. But when he finally made his choice, we didn't look back. We helped him move forward.

My youngest? Well... he's still young enough that his big decisions are between Peter Piper Pizza or Papa Johns. But still, decisions are decisions.

And the older we get, the heavier these decisions feel. But that doesn't mean they're supposed to be perfect. We think decisions are about control. About mapping every variable and predicting every ripple. But the truth is, we treat decisions like chess moves, thinking if we plan ten steps ahead, we'll outsmart life. But most of the time? Life flips the board. And you're not left with the perfect plan; you're left with the present moment. The only thing that ever really existed. We're not making perfect choices; we're co-creating outcomes. When you decide something with full alignment; when it's rooted in your values, your peace, your present truth, you're not just choosing. You're saying to the Universe: "I'm here. I'm listening. Let's build this together."

And that energy? It opens doors. Even if the path doesn't unfold the way you imagined. Even if you have to pivot later. The decision itself becomes sacred, not because it was flawless, but because it was *honest.* You didn't freeze. You didn't wait for permission. You chose. And that's how momentum starts.

One of the hardest parts of choosing something is what comes after. The pressure to stick with it. The guilt that says, *"Well, you chose this. Now deal with it."* But here's the truth I had to learn the hard way: You don't owe loyalty to a decision that no longer serves who you're becoming.

We evolve. We learn. We grow into new clarity. And the version of you who made that choice? She did her best. She made the call based on who she was, what she knew, and what she needed. That's not failure. That's movement. "But what if I choose wrong again?" Then you'll do what you've always done. You'll learn. You'll pivot. You'll live. Not everything has to be forever to be worth it. I used to stay in situations way too long, jobs, relationships, even business decisions, just because I didn't want to look like I gave up. But staying stuck in something just to prove you're not a quitter? That's not strength. That's fear, dressed up as discipline. And fear makes terrible life plans. Real strength is knowing when it's time to shift. And trusting yourself enough to do it.

I've made decisions that didn't lead where I thought they would. I've said yes to things that broke my heart. I've walked down paths that looked promising and ended up feeling like detours. But each time, I came back to the same truth: The decision wasn't wrong. The facts just changed. What I knew then is not what I know now. And with every new truth, every new awareness, I gain the power to choose again. That's the work. Not punishing yourself. Not trying to rewind. But choosing again, with more wisdom this time. Current wisdom. Wisdom that can change.

We punish ourselves for not being able to predict the future. We judge *past* versions of ourselves with the clarity we have *now.* But that's not fair and it's not kind. The truth is, once you make a decision, the other one ceases to exist. That version of reality no longer lives here.

I tell my kids this all the time:
Once we make a decision, based on the information we have and the alignment we feel right now, that other option? It disappears.

That path is no longer lit. It's no longer visible. And sure, if we need to pivot later, we can. Of course. But that's because the circumstances changed. Not because we made the "wrong" call. I don't really buy into the whole "hindsight is 20/20" thing anymore. Yes, clarity can come later...but often? That clarity *only* came because we took the path we did. Because we lived it. Because we showed up to it. Because we learned what we were meant to learn. So stop comparing your current life to a hypothetical one that doesn't exist. Stop looking back with shame in your eyes.

You chose. You learned. You grew. And if a new path is needed, you'll choose again. Not from guilt. But from growth.

We don't need to strive for perfection. We need to build our muscle of self-trust. Because a person who trusts themselves can walk any road with integrity. They can pivot. They can learn. They can say, *"That choice served me... until it didn't."* And then? They make the next one. No guilt. No shame. No punishment. Just evolution.

YOU ARE NOT BEHIND. You're just building in real time.

Reflection

- What decisions are you still punishing yourself for?

- If you could talk to the version of you who made that choice, what would you say?

- What facts have changed since then?

- What new choices do you have now?

Affirmation

I do not need a perfect path. I need a present one. I trust myself to decide, pivot, and move forward, without punishment. Every choice is a step. Every step is growth.

Chapter Sixteen

The Universe Is For You

When you stop demanding perfection from yourself, something strange begins to happen: You start making room for grace and welcoming divine timing. You make space for the kind of outcomes you can't spreadsheet your way into. Because once you realize your decisions aren't about controlling life... you're free to co-create with it. You stop asking, "Did I choose wrong?" and start *wondering, "What if this delay is a detour with a purpose?"* And that's when the shift begins. It's the moment you stop treating life like a test and start trusting that the Universe is in the room *with* you. Not grading your moves, but guiding them and supporting them.

I used to believe the Universe was testing me. Every setback felt like punishment. Every "no" felt like rejection. Every hard season felt like proof that I wasn't doing it right. That I had missed something. That maybe I wasn't cut out for the big, beautiful life I dreamed about. But I've since learned something deeper: The Universe isn't testing you. It's positioning you.

The Universe isn't here to see if you'll break. It's here to help you become unshakable.

The shifts you're going through aren't random. Not at all. You're being moved, not because you're failing, but because your soul is ready to grow. And sometimes that growth doesn't look like ease. It looks like shedding. It looks like stillness. It looks like the hallway between the version of you who's tired of suffering... and the version who's finally ready to receive. It's the caterpillar turning to goo before emerging as a butterfly. Not everything that hurts is a punishment. Not every delay is a denial. Sometimes the detour is the direction.

We've been conditioned to believe in a version of "alignment" that looks like everything flowing perfectly, you know, no obstacles, no resistance, and no wrong turns. But alignment isn't about the absence of difficulty. It's about what you choose to believe in the middle of it. Trusting the Universe when everything's working out is easy. But when you're trusting it when nothing makes sense, when you're sitting in the middle of a breakdown, a betrayal, or a burnout, that's the work. The real work. It's brushing your teeth while you silently cry. It's applying for something even after the last three said no. It's making dinner while your bank account groans. It's setting your alarm even when you're not sure why you're still trying. It's moving forward with hope.

That's trust. Not blind optimism or spiritual bypassing. Just you, showing up, tender, tired, and still open. And the Universe meets that energy. Every time. Now don't get me wrong. You don't have to love the pain. You definitely don't have to pretend it's not hard. But you can hold on to the truth that something is working *for* you, even if you can't see it yet. I keep coming back to my awareness and start paying attention to what's shifting inside me. I notice the way my perspective softens. The way my tolerance for inauthenticity shrinks. The way I stop forcing what isn't mine.

That is the Universe. *That* is the shift. *That* is the sign. And speaking of signs, I look for those, too.

{Side note: I'm sure this won't come as a surprise, but I don't believe in coincidence. I think everything has meaning if you are open enough to seek it. Every time I see 11:11 on the clock, you'd better believe I'm treating it like a portal and thanking the Universe for everything and "placing my order" for more. (My favorite thing is that our kids do it now, too!)

And even though we live in the desert, I'm looking up the spiritual meaning every time a coyote crosses my path, or a bird catches our eye, when my ear starts ringing, a butterfly flutters by, a ladybug lands on me, a lizard or a bee comes to say hello, if there's a spider in the house, (which I also don't kill, just relocate) – it doesn't matter what it is, if it's out of the "norm", I'm looking it up. I try to see how it applies to me in that moment.}

There were times I felt like the Universe had gone silent. I remember one night in particular. I had just walked out of a client session, one of those where everything technically went right, but I still walked out feeling empty. I got in my car, shut the door, and the silence was deafening. No messages. No signs. No validation. And still, something in me whispered, *"You're not lost. You're being rerouted."* I didn't believe it at first. I wanted a neon sign, not a whisper. But looking back, that whisper was the sign and I had to trust.

Sometimes the doors don't open because what's on the other side isn't ready for you. Sometimes you're not ready for it. Sometimes, the Universe is doing work on your behalf behind the scenes, and the delay is the protection. I've stopped asking, *"Why is this happening to me?"* And started asking, *"Why is this happening FOR me?"* (Or what is this preparing me for?) That question changes everything. It gets you out of victim mode and into co-creation. It reminds you that you're not just floating through life waiting to be chosen.

You are active in your becoming. And the Universe is your partner and your supporter, not your punisher. I feel like the sooner we realize that the easier it becomes. The Universe *wants* to create *with* you.

***

I know I touched upon it earlier, but I want to give you a little more insight. We had lived in our rental home for almost ten years. It was where we raised our kids. Built our routines. Held garage talks. It was ours. And then, the owners decided to sell while the market was high. I don't blame them, but it felt like everything we built was being ripped away from us. We had less than two months to get out. Ten years, packed and gone in under sixty days. The rental market was brutal. Prices were wild. We were devastated. We scrambled to find something, literally anything to make it work. We were just trying to survive it. We ended up finding a house that was quirky, imperfect, and hot as hell (literally, no central air in the middle of a Southwest summer). It was so hard, and even though we *had* to move, there were still moments (dark, heavy ones) where I thought, *"Why is this happening to us?"* We didn't ask for this chaos. We weren't trying to start over. We just wanted to survive. And yet somehow, surviving felt like we were failing. That's the part no one talks about. The doubt that creeps in even when you're doing your best.

We moved in at the end of June. It was so. Freakin. Hot. We tried to smile through it for the kids. The initial few days there ended up being a bit of a disaster. Once we stocked our cabinets with food, there were ants everywhere. The hot water heater wouldn't light. The water hadn't even been turned on by the rental company. Come to find out none of the required inspections were completed. We felt punished. Forsaken. Exhausted. It didn't seem fair.

We cried. All of us. But we pushed through.

After we realized the chaos when we moved in, we had no choice but to stay at my parents' house for a few days before heading to Salt Lake City for our daughter's Regional ID Camp for soccer. A trip that was planned for months, before we knew where our housing situation would land us. We didn't know how we were going to make it. We were nearly out of money because of the move, the deposits, the much—much higher rent, but still decided we had to lead with our values. What are we fighting for? This opportunity for our daughter. A vacation for our family. A way to get out and leave the troubles of the new rental. A change of pace. A way of separating from the pain we were engulfed in. The timing of that trip was *for* us. We made the best of it, eating Sam's Club pizza and hotdogs, doing our best to keep it together. Going to parks. Finding cheap things to do and explore. We didn't have a plan. We didn't know how we were going to manage this new payment. And then... a post. Koko put something up on Facebook, seeing if anyone needed marketing help. That post (random and hopeful) landed us an interview with a local cannabis shop when we got back.

We were hired on the spot. Suddenly, things didn't feel quite so desperate. Suddenly, that quirky house became a sanctuary. I carved out a space for my boudoir studio. I started building it up. We had room to grow. We had room to breathe. And month-to-month money turned into month-to-month with a little extra.

The Universe had shaken us out of survival. It whispered time and time again to rise up. It presented opportunities for us to grow, but we were comfortable in our old house and familiar situation, so we didn't budge. We were content, sure, but not really *growing*. Comfortably stagnant. Finally, like a fed-up parent, it said, *"Enough. It's time to move forward."* The Universe could no longer operate in subtlety and wait for us to catch on. So it shoved...and we finally moved.

That moment, the forced move, the panic, the tears, it was never punishment. It was the divine interruption we didn't know we needed.

I no longer wait for everything to feel easy before I trust the path. I trust it while my knees shake. I trust it while I'm crying. I trust it even when I'm mad about it. Because trust isn't just a feeling, it's a decision. And that decision is the thing that opens the next door.

There are still days I doubt. Days when I forget. Days I need to just sit in the car or cry in the shower or have a full-on garage session just to release. But every time, I find my way back to this knowing:

The Universe is not neutral. It's not indifferent. It's for me and it's for you. Always.

You are being called deeper. You are being asked to show up for yourself even when no one else claps. You are being invited to trust what you can't yet see. And I know that's scary. I know that feels like a free fall sometimes. But if you're here, still reading, still healing, still trying, that means you've already survived everything you once feared. And it's okay if you've lost it right now. If you can't see the light. If you can't climb your way out. You will. You will find it again.

So maybe the Universe isn't testing you. Maybe it's reminding you. That you're worthy. That you're powerful. That you're on time. That you've never been alone in this.

The Universe is not behind you, catching your fall. It's ahead of you, building your landing. You have to stop praying for open doors if you're not willing to walk the hallway. You have to put in some effort as you're asking for the life you desire. You have to show up. It's like begging the Universe to win the lottery, but you've never bought a ticket. Do you think you're just going to magically stumble across the Willy Wonka bar?

The Universe is not against you. You don't have to prove your worth. You don't have to hustle for your healing. You don't have to earn your desires. You get to receive. You get to rest. You get to trust. Because the truth is simple, even if it takes time to believe: The Universe is for you. The Universe is for you. The Universe is for you.

Read it again. Whisper it to yourself. Write it on your mirror. Tattoo it to your mind. Now go live like it.

Reflection:

Think about a time you thought everything was falling apart, but it was really falling into place.

- What "detour" ended up becoming the most aligned path?

- What felt like a breakdown, but turned into a breakthrough?

- What moments felt like devastation but became a doorway?

Let me drive this home. The Universe isn't out to break you. It's trying to build you. And it's doing a damn good job. Something else to consider, the Universe doesn't just speak through milestones or breakthroughs. Sometimes, it whispers to you through stillness. Through the pause. Through the fog. There's a lesson in the days that feel off. The ones where nothing is technically wrong... but nothing feels quite right either. These days aren't a setback. They're a signal.

Because when you're tuned into trust, even the grey has something to teach you.

What would you do differently if you believed, without a doubt, that the Universe was on your side today?

CHAPTER SEVENTEEN

GREY DAYS AND ALIGNMENT

Have you ever had a day that just felt... off? Like you couldn't fully arrive for it. Where little annoyances felt impossible to manage and you felt overly sensitive for no clear reason?

I call them Grey Days.

It's the kind of day that feels like it's lost its vibrancy...like someone dimmed the world just a bit, and we don't have the remote to turn it back up. You can't quite name what's wrong. There's no clear trigger. Nothing dramatic. And yet... you just don't feel like yourself. You can't arrive at happiness. You can't get into your body. You can't fake the joy, because it's not there.

And you start wondering what's wrong with you. Are you just lazy? Are you just not trying hard enough?

That's when the inner dialogue ramps up:
"You should be doing more."
"Other people don't fall apart over nothing." "Seriously, get it together."

It's subtle, but relentless. And if you're not paying attention, that voice becomes the loudest thing in the room. That voice convinces you the grey is your fault instead of a flag.

Sometimes gratitude works. Sometimes journaling or mindfulness helps. Sometimes a nap resets your nervous system. And sometimes... nothing works. And that's okay, too.

Not every breakdown looks like chaos. Sometimes it's just that feeling where everything is off and you can't explain why. You're not crying. You're not screaming. You're just... gone. You go through the motions, but nothing sticks. You make the coffee, but it doesn't taste right. You forget why you walked into the room. You try to shake it off, but the fog doesn't lift.

You're not sad enough to cry. Not tired enough to sleep. You're just... floating. Half here. Half somewhere else. Like you're watching your life through glass. I imagine it's like living underwater. Everything's slowed down, muffled, just out of reach. Your body's present, but your spirit called in sick.

You're technically "doing the thing"...but it's like going through the motions with no soundtrack, no spark, no sense of being in it.

And the worst part? You still expect yourself to function.

You keep stacking things on your to-do list, like maybe if you get enough done, the feeling will go away. You keep smiling through it. You answer texts. You show up. You try to be "on." But inside, you're just waiting for the day to end so you can disappear into bed and hope you feel different tomorrow.

That's the trap, isn't it? Feeling like you don't have the right to slow down unless you're falling apart. Like it's only valid to rest if you're sick or sobbing.

But what about when your soul is just... tired? What about when you're running on fumes, but nobody can tell, because you've gotten so good at pretending you're fine?

Grey Days don't always come with warning signs. They don't announce themselves like breakdowns do. They sneak in quiet. They sit heavy. They mess with your appetite, your patience, your focus. You start feeling like a problem that needs solving.

But maybe the real problem is how hard you try to ignore it.

What if you didn't? What if you just said, "Okay. This is a grey day. I'm not going to try to outrun it today." What would change?

What if you let the day be slow, weird, and gentle? What if you canceled the plans, wore the hoodie, scrolled without guilt, or just stared at the ceiling and didn't apologize for it?

What if the only thing that needed to get done today... was you softening?

Giving yourself a day (or two) to sit in it. Not fixing, or pushing, or pressuring. Not pretending to be more okay than you are. Just softening. Just noticing. Just not bulldozing through the fog like it owes you clarity. Because maybe it doesn't owe you anything. Maybe it's just showing up to tell you something you've been too busy to hear.

Sometimes the fog is the message. It's one of the ways the Universe tries to get our attention, to hint that we need to chill out a bit. The grey isn't the breakdown, it's the buffer. The pause before your body breaks. The warning before burnout.

You can cancel the plans. You can put your phone on Do Not Disturb. You can binge dumb TV in the same hoodie all day. You can take a damn nap.

And maybe you're thinking, "That sounds nice, but I don't get to slow down. I have kids. Deadlines. A house to run."

I hear you.

Sometimes the whole world won't stop for your nervous system. But maybe you can. Just a little. The dishes will be there tomorrow. The laundry can wait another day. Maybe it's not a full pause, but a softer approach. One less expectation. One less item on your to do list. Even a 5% slowdown is still a shift. And sometimes, that's all it takes to breathe again. And maybe nothing's wrong... except your refusal to slow down.

Remember, Grey Days don't always announce themselves. You wake up with a weight in your chest. You scroll and feel disconnected from everything. Is it your mood? Or are you just overdue for a damn break?

Your to-do list feels impossible. You overthink a comment someone made yesterday. You try to snap out of it, but can't quite get there. And that's the thing: You can't fix what you haven't named.

If you don't recognize it's a Grey Day, it just feels like a bad mood. Like you're failing at life. Like maybe something's wrong with you.

But when you say it out loud..."This is a Grey Day", and you take back control. You stop trying to chase joy that won't land. You stop spiraling about why you feel "off." You stop judging your energy.

And instead, you sit with it. You say, "Okay. This is one of those days. We're going to get through it. That's the goal today: through."

It doesn't mean you give up. It means you give grace. You lower the bar. You drink water. You turn the music on low or find a new audiobook and fold the laundry slowly. You cancel what doesn't feel urgent. You don't perform. You just be. You ride the wave without trying to control it. That's the art of the Grey Day. Awareness and acceptance.

Maybe sometimes... it's not you in the grey. It's your partner. Your child. A coworker. A friend. And suddenly you're standing in the blast radius of their grey storm, wondering: "What did I do?" "Did I mess something up?" "Why are they acting this way toward me?"

Here's the reminder that'll save you a lot of suffering: It's not always about you.

Someone else's mood isn't proof of your failure. Someone else's silence doesn't mean you're being punished. Someone else's edge isn't always your responsibility.

When someone is projecting, it's not always obvious. It might come off as snippy, distant, or passive aggressive. It might look like withdrawal, angry sarcasm, or irritation.

Your initial reaction is that you might want to fix it. Or maybe you'll want to retreat. Hell, you might want to lash back.

But before you react, try asking: "Is this mine to carry?" "Or is this their grey day speaking?"

This doesn't mean you let people treat you poorly. It means you pause long enough to decide what's yours and what isn't.

Some of the kindest things you can offer someone in the grey are simple: A quiet room and their favorite drink. A "take your time" or a "no pressure" or even a simple "I'm here." Sometimes that's all they needed. Not your solution. Just your presence.

As I'm writing this... I'm coming off a grey day. A day where I woke up with nothing in the tank. Where I was exhausted but didn't sleep poorly. Where I was emotionally raw but couldn't quite explain why. I was frustrated with myself because I wasn't in a joyful place. And worse...I know better. I've had this happen SO many times that I should be able to reign it in. And yet... I had to remind myself again:

This is just a grey day. It doesn't need to be fixed. It just needs to be named.

Now that I know what these days are, our whole family is better at giving grace when one of us is in it. What I wish more people understood is this: There may not be a cause. Not a clear one, anyway. It might be burnout. It might be overwhelm. It might be something your body remembers even when your brain doesn't.

When there's no obvious reason, that alone may be the sign. It's not a failure. It's not a flaw. It's just a subtle flag. That whisper. Your body saying, "Hey... I need a minute."

And when the people around you understand that (and especially when you understand it) the whole atmosphere changes. It becomes gentler. Less reactive.

A grey day might actually be a gift. That little nudge from the Universe: "Slow down. You're running on fumes."

The Universe will whisper at first. It'll be that quiet nudge, the off energy, the little drop in motivation. But it can only speak subtly for so long. If you ignore it too many times, it'll bring the hammer. The shutdown. The breakdown. The moment where you are forced to listen.

So maybe grey days are the grace before the fall. The sacred tap on the shoulder that says, "Hey... this matters."

And if you try to power through... If you push and perform and pretend... Those grey days are going to start to multiply, until burnout becomes your baseline.

But if you can acknowledge it... If you can name it... If you can honor it... If you can give yourself grace, you'll often find your mind, body, and soul just needed a sick day.

Please, allow for it. This isn't the day to demand productivity. This is the day for soft clothes, warm drinks, and gentle shows. This is the day for naps and pet snuggles, deep breaths and slow, mindless movement. Let self-care be your medicine. Let rest be your healer. Let the grey be your guide and not your enemy.

Because sometimes the truest kind of healing starts with: "Today, I'm doing less. And that's enough."

Alignment Isn't Always Loud

If your grey days start becoming the norm for you, then there's something else that is missing. It's not just about rest anymore. It's about alignment. Because when you wake up in the fog more often than not or when the heaviness stops being temporary and starts feeling like your baseline, it's no longer just a low moment. It's a sign. A slow leak. A buildup. A drift away from the life you actually want to be living.

That's what happened to us. Not overnight. Not in crisis. It crept in through busyness. Through overcommitment. Through too many quiet yeses to things that didn't actually serve us.

And by the time we realized it... we weren't just tired. We were lost in it.

Our schedule's been overrun by commitments we didn't mean to make. Actually, we *did* mean to make them, but they were introduced so slowly, the small things didn't seem like they'd add up the way they had. Soccer had taken over, and somewhere along the way, our summer was disappearing.

Last night, sitting in the garage, the place where truth always seems to break open, I looked at Koko and said it out loud: "We are way out of alignment." And the thing is? Neither of us argued. Because we knew.

The garage is our sanctuary, but even that space had started to reflect the chaos. Cluttered. Unfinished. Drained. Boxes from the move still half-unpacked. The pool table turned storage hub. Just sitting there, like a metaphor for everything we keep putting off. Every "undone" thing we keep stepping around. Frames scattered across the air hockey table, waiting for a wall that hasn't been chosen. Those black-and-yellow Christmas bins stacked in the middle like caution tape for our energy. The workout corner? Covered in dust, because we've barely had the energy to breathe, let alone lift. The gold string of lights that once wrapped the space in warmth now hangs like a tangled sculpture off the pull-up machine. I call it our accidental art installation; it's my way of putting a band-aid over it. I try to laugh about it, knowing that I *should* be doing something about it. There are only two chairs in the whole space: A rocking chair we've had since our oldest was a baby, and a yellow cushioned one we stole from the kitchen. A small stool acts as our table, holding our cannabis tools, a lighter, and my sippy (that metal water bottle that somehow follows me everywhere). An incense burner is propped on the unused trash can. And in the air, a mix of incense and yesterday's session, a soft reminder of the conversations from last night.

The Home Glow playlist hums in the background, familiar enough to hold my brain open while the rest of me catches up. This is where we come to feel. To breathe. To name what's been quietly unraveling inside us.

This is what being out of alignment looks like. It's not always chaos. It's not always a dramatic wake-up call. Sometimes it's just quiet resignation. Sometimes it's just your body aching for rest. Sometimes it's the realization that you're alive... but not *living*. And when you don't catch it in time? You hit the breaking point.

And no, that's not a failure. That's your body's emergency broadcast system. It's your last line of defense. The only way it knows how to scream:

"ENOUGH."

The breaking point is your soul hitting the brakes while your ego is still gunning the gas. It's the body saying, *"You didn't listen to the whispers. So here's the roar."* Lately, I've said it more than once, "I'm drowning." And every time, I *smiled* while I said it. Performing wellness. Convincing myself I was fine. That playful tone? That was my ego saying, *"You made your bed, now lie in it."* But I wasn't fine. Not even close.

Koko and I are usually on the same page. Wildly connected. We rarely fight, rarely argue, rarely even snap at each other. And that should've been the first clue. Because lately? We've been off. Disconnected. Worn down. Unsaid things piling up like dirty dishes. Last night, he finally said it out loud: "This isn't the life we planned." And I knew exactly what he meant.

We've been in our new rental for four months, and it doesn't feel like home. How could it? We don't live there, we just rotate through it. Sleep. Shower. Survive. Repeat. The walls are bare. The kitchen's always cluttered. We don't have time or energy to keep up with the mess. We've turned this supposed dream era into a pressure cooker.

We've become prisoners of our own making. Trapped in a cycle of "just one more thing." One more obligation. One more commitment. One more sacrifice. He looked at me, and for the first time in a long time, I saw it: His breaking point.

So we sat in it. Hand in hand. And we said the things. The hard things. The real things. How it wasn't supposed to feel like this. How we lost control of the schedule, the energy, the connection. How we needed to take it all back.

We started canceling. Realigning. And yes, it hurt. It goes right along with having the difficult conversation. I had to tell my daughter we wouldn't be joining the last-minute summer soccer trip that was starting to be planned. She was understandably upset. She didn't want to talk in the car like usual. No banter. No music suggestions. Just silence. Just disappointment. She looked out the window and said, "Can you just drop me off?" And I did. Part of me wanted to soften the blow. To explain. To make it okay for her. But I'm learning that not every moment needs rescuing. Sometimes love means holding space for their disappointment, and trusting they'll come back when they're ready.

On the drive home, I called my mom, like I do every morning. I told her how we needed to realign. How we were at our breaking point. How I *knew* in my body that I wasn't on the right path, and I was making changes now. And then...something happened and everything inside me stilled. A hawk soared across my windshield. She was Massive. Poised. Present. She landed on a streetlight in front of me and locked eyes. Then she called out. Loud. On purpose. Over and over. And right then, this quiet knowing washed over me: *"This is the turning point."* I looked it up later:

"When the hawk speaks, you're meant to listen. It could be interpreted as your soul—or even your ancestors—saying: 'The shift starts now. Stay in your truth. Let your voice lead. Protect your peace like a hunter protects its focus.'" I swear that bird wasn't just watching me, it was *witnessing* me. Marking the moment I stopped spiraling and started choosing alignment.

Here's the truth: **Alignment doesn't always feel good at first.** It doesn't feel like peace right away. Sometimes it feels like grief. Like chaos. Like disappointing the people you love. But it's not misalignment, it's *detox*. It's the withdrawal symptoms from a life built on obligation. It's the ache of realizing how long you've been white knuckling everything. It's the discomfort of taking off the mask you didn't know you'd been wearing.

Realignment requires disruption. When you've been living on everyone else's schedule, saying "yes" out of habit, pushing through instead of tuning in. Of course, the reset feels jarring. Of course, your nervous system freaks out when you start saying no. But that's the thing about healing: It doesn't feel like healing at first. It feels like falling apart. Until it doesn't. Until the space clears. Until the quiet softens. Until your home starts to feel like home again. Until you're sitting in the garage, not unraveling, but laughing. Talking about nothing and everything. Being present again. That's alignment. Not just the absence of stress, but the presence of self.

One thing that's good to acknowledge is your body typically knows you're out of alignment before your brain does. Some things to pay attention to include snapping over small things, avoiding everything that once felt easy, feeling disconnected from joy, noticing resentment toward the calendar, and/or aching for time to just be. These aren't flaws. They're signals. And the more we ignore them, the louder they get - until we can't suppress them anymore.

Reflection

- What does stress feel like in your body?

- How can you recognize the signs earlier?

- What commitments are currently draining you?

- Where have you been choosing peacekeeping over peacemaking?

- What would it look like to disappoint others in order to honor yourself?

Affirmation

I am allowed to change direction. I trust my body to guide me back to alignment. It's safe to rest. It's safe to reset. It's safe to return to myself. And if I need to burn it all down to rebuild...so be it.

But it's not just your schedule that can wear you down. Sometimes, it's who you've been trying to be. Sometimes, the misalignment isn't in your calendar. It's in your connections. Not because you don't love your people. But because you've been trying to belong in places that don't see the full version of you.

You can cancel the meetings, clear the schedule, reclaim your time, but what about the weight of trying to be what you're not? What about the loneliness that creeps in even when you're surrounded? What about the quiet ache of being known, but not quite understood?

This is the next piece of the healing: Letting go of the idea that closeness has to be constant. That friendship has to be loud to be loyal. That love only counts if it shows up daily. Because some of us love in *seasons*. Some of us connect in waves. Some of us don't need a tribe, we need truth.

This next chapter is for you. For the ones who show up deeply, even if not always visibly. For the ones who love fiercely... just not on demand. When I think about alignment now, I don't just think about work or family or schedule. I think about connection. About friendships. About the way we show up for others, and how we let them show up for us.

Because as I've realigned every other part of my life...I've had to look at where I fit (or don't fit) in the lives of others. And that's brought up some truth I didn't expect. The truth is: I've never been the center of the circle. Not the go-to. Not the group chat friend. Not the one people rearrange their calendars for. And for a long time, that hurt. But now? Now I understand. Now I see it not as a flaw, but as a frequency. One that doesn't need to be loud to be real.

And maybe...that's what alignment really is. Finally fitting into your own rhythm, instead of forcing someone else's.

CHAPTER EIGHTEEN

THE OUTSIDER FRIEND

I'm not the "group chat" friend. I'm not the girl with the tight-knit tribe or the go-to invitee for wine nights and birthday trips. I don't have a standing girls' night or a thread that's always buzzing. I'm the outsider friend. Not in a sad way, just in a true way. Honestly, my life doesn't allow for constant connection. My nervous system doesn't either. But I love deeply. I show up fiercely. I see people. And I've made peace with not fitting the mold. My life is loud. Busy. Full. I'm a mom of three. A coach. A business owner. A healer. A creator. And I don't always have space to be the everyday friend. I don't show up consistently in texts or calls. I miss birthdays. I forget to respond. I love you...and I'm still overwhelmed.

I think it's more honest to say I show up in seasons. In eras. In the moments that matter, and sometimes, that's all I can manage. But it doesn't mean I don't care. It just means I'm human. With a finite amount of capacity. And a nervous system that's already running at full tilt most days.

I was bullied relentlessly in elementary school and middle school. Not just teased but picked apart. Crooked teeth. Hair that wasn't curly or straight, just thin, hard to manage, always *wrong*. Too white in our Hispanic community to fully fit in. Too quiet to push back. Too sensitive to pretend it didn't hurt. I wore the wrong clothes. I didn't have the brands the other girls had. And even when I tried to blend in, I stood out, but not in the way I wanted. I had one constant friend back then. She was my safe space. The kind of friend who never made me feel like too much or not enough. She just let me be. No pressure. No performance. Just presence. We ended up at different middle schools, and eventually, she moved to California. And when she left, it felt like my anchor left with her.

She was and still is vibrant. She's laughter and love wrapped in human form. One of the funniest, "life of the party" girls you'll ever meet. The kind of person people naturally gather around. The boys loved her growing up. The other kids gravitated to her like sunlight. And yet... she never made me feel like I had to compete with that energy. She let me be soft in her shine. Even now, decades later, we're not in constant contact. Life has gotten louder, busier, more complex. I fall off the map regularly, buried under work and kids and the general chaos of this season. But she's still there. A quiet hum in the background of my life. Steady. Constant. An auntie to my kids. Always a phone call away. Never making me feel bad for surviving.

She just... gets it.

And even though we don't talk as often, I still feel that thread between us. Like no matter how much time passes, we could pick up the conversation right where we left off. That kind of friendship is rare. And I know how lucky I am to have it.

There was one friend in eighth grade I adored, someone who was funny and magnetic, and let's be honest, popular. And, somehow, still chose to be close with me. And even though she never made me feel small... I made myself small anyway. I was terrified that *I* would make *her* look bad. That being friends with me would drag down her social value. You know how middle school is. So I tried to earn my place. Tried not to take up too much space. Tried to be grateful for her presence, while quietly believing I didn't deserve it. She was a real friend. I know that now. Self-worth and the constant feeling that I wasn't enough was likely the quiet dagger that separated us as we moved into high school. And even though we've only kept up through the occasional Facebook comment or quiet like, I still cheer her on from afar. And I believe, deep down, that she's still cheering for me too.

Now, I have a small village of close friends. They aren't all connected either. Not a group chat. Not a weekly brunch crew. Just a handful of people who get me. Who love me as I am. Who don't require constant check-ins to know they matter, or to remind me that I do. But even now, I'm not the all-the-time, everyday friend. And finally? I understand that about myself.

I rarely answer the phone. I almost never check messages right away. I forget to watch the videos I get sent (Sorry, guys—really, I mean it). And for a long time, I felt shame about that. I felt like I was failing the "rules" of friendship. Like I wasn't doing it right because I didn't *feel* available all the time. But now I know the truth: It's not because I don't care. It's because I care deeply, but my bandwidth is limited. I try to really show up when it matters. I drop in when something feels heavy. I speak truth when I know you're spiraling. And when I *do* connect, it's real. Present. Undiluted. My friendships are fewer, but richer now. There's no performance. No pressure to keep up appearances or stay on-script. We don't talk every day, but when we do, it lands. It fills. It restores.

They understand that I'm stretched thin, often overbooked, sometimes missing, but never gone. And I trust them enough to not take my silence as disconnection. Just space. That's the kind of friendship I crave. That's the kind of friendship I offer.

I used to think being the outsider meant something was wrong with me. Like I wasn't chosen. Like I didn't belong. But I see it differently now. I was always meant to be the outsider. Not because I wasn't worthy of being in the group...But because I was meant to be the bridge. The one who moved between people and seasons. The one who could see the bigger picture. The one who didn't need the spotlight to light others up. I've been the bridge between friend groups. The bridge between who you are and who you're becoming. The bridge back to yourself when the noise gets too loud. And it took years of healing to see that as a gift. To not just be okay with it, but to honor it. To understand that "outsider" isn't a wound. It's a role. A calling. A way of moving through the world with purpose, even when it feels like you're moving alone.

Being the outsider friend holds more value than you can possibly imagine. You don't need to be the main character to be magnetic. You don't need the group chat to be grounded. You can exist exactly as you are, quiet, observant, tender, true... And *still* be the reason someone feels seen. Still be the echo that reminds them they matter. Still be the gentle force that brings people back to themselves. That's your superpower. And it's more than enough.

So, trust me. You don't have to be in the group photo to matter. You don't have to show up every day to be a safe place. You don't have to perform connection to prove you care.

You are allowed to be the outsider. The bridge. The steady hand. The quiet hum of love that never needs a spotlight. Your presence really is powerful, even when it's subtle. Your friendship is real, even when it's seasonal. And the way you love, imperfectly, intermittently, *intentionally*...is still enough. We're so wired to believe that closeness comes from constant connection. That being a good friend means always being available, always responding, always plugged in. But that's not the truth. Closeness doesn't require constant noise. You don't need to be everywhere to mean everything. But when you start measuring your worth by digital echoes...you forget how deeply your presence lands in real life.

Reflection

- Where have you felt like an outsider in your relationships?

- What would it feel like to release the pressure to perform connection?

- Who in your life loves you *without needing all of you, all the time*?

Don't allow yourself to feel the need to constantly check in or scroll Facebook. Connection doesn't live in the scroll. The same phone that brings people into your life...can also be the thing that pulls *you* away from your own. But before we blame the phone, let's talk about what we're feeding ourselves through it. Let's talk about how we use it, why we reach for it, and what it's really costing us. Because the phone isn't really the problem. Your phone diet is.

CHAPTER NINETEEN

THE PHONE ISN'T THE PROBLEM, YOUR PHONE DIET IS

You keep blaming your phone for your burnout, your distraction, your low mood, but it's not the phone. It's what you're feeding yourself every time you open it. Just like your body responds to the food you eat, your mind responds to the content you consume. Think about what's really on your mental plate: comparison, anxiety, drama, urgency, overstimulation. And you're snacking on it **all day long**. You may have already known it, or maybe you're just learning you're just on a toxic phone diet. We scroll through highlight reels and curated identities. We drown in a sea of perfection and self-help that makes us feel like we're never doing enough. Then we blame the phone, when the truth is... your phone is just a mirror.

What are you feeding your mind? Ask yourself: Who are you following? How do you feel after consuming their content? Are you opening your phone to connect or to escape? Our phones reflect our inner world. If you're always doom scrolling or checking in on people who trigger self-doubt, you're creating a feedback loop of fear, shame, and not-enoughness. You don't need to go off the grid, you need a digital detox of the soul.

I'd encourage you to start filtering your phone content the same way you would clear your home of clutter. Ask: Does this give me energy, or take it? Does this inspire me, or make me question myself? Am I consuming out of intention or out of habit? (That last one is my personal favorite!) This isn't about perfection. It's about awareness. Unfollow the influencers that push hustle as self-worth. Mute the accounts that leave you feeling hollow. Choose what you want to see. Reclaim your feed, and you reclaim your energy.

 You don't need to respond to every DM. You don't need to be available all the time. You don't need to keep people around out of guilt. You are allowed to create space between you and what drains you. Here are some steps that have helped me. Start with killing non-essential notifications. Then delete the apps that suck your time and joy. I ditched games... not because I'm above them, but because they were always whispering, 'Just one more level.' (Spoiler: it's never just one more.) The more noise I removed, the more space I made. You don't realize how often you're beckoned back to your phone. It happens so frequently, and out of habit, we draw our phone back up to our face. One ping becomes ten minutes lost. We tell ourselves, "I'm just checking the time," but somehow end up deep in reels without even realizing it. The pull is designed. The spiral is intentional. Without even realizing, you just lost another 10 minutes. I caught myself checking IG between brushing my teeth and spitting out the toothpaste. That's how automatic it had become. Not joy. Not connection. Just habit. It happens in a hurry- and they are SO good at knowing what will draw us in and keep watching just a little longer.

Start following people who speak to your soul, not to your shame. ←-PAY ATTENTION HERE.

This is easily the most impactful if you find yourself struggling to get away from your phone. Once you start becoming aware, you'll start to know the difference. The soul-speakers? They just hit different. They remind you of who you *are*, not who you should be. They don't sell you a glow-up you didn't ask for. They whisper truth back to the parts of you that forgot. Their posts feel like a hand on your shoulder, not a finger pointing at everything you're not doing "right". If you leave someone's page feeling like you're not doing enough, being enough, healing fast enough, that's a good time to pause. That's when we mute. Unfollow. Recalibrate. We live in a world where comparison has become part of our morning coffee routine. We scroll ourselves into shame spirals and call it "inspiration." But here's the truth: inspiration should feel expansive. Not like a punch in the gut. Curate your feed like you'd curate your home...intentionally, gently, with the kind of energy you want to come home to. But here's the thing, just because it's difficult doesn't mean it's not worth it. I try to treat my phone like a tool, not a temptation. I don't let it decide how I feel about my day before I've even gotten out of bed. I post my intention, then I put it down. That's the deal. No messages. No DMs. No clicking into apps "just for a second." Because again, we both know...it's never just a second.

That one choice changes the whole tone of my morning. It reminds me: *I get to be the one who sets the energy today.* Not the algorithm. Not the chat. Not someone else's emergency. If you're not there yet, that's okay. You don't have to copy what I do. But maybe you leave your phone in another room for the first 10–20 minutes. Maybe you swap scrolling for stretching. Maybe you meet yourself first, before the world gets a chance to. There's no perfect way to do it. But I promise, there's power in pausing before you plug back in.

Clear your home screen of apps. This is one of the biggest game changers I've done. When your home screen is blank, you aren't beckoned by the little numbers of notifications you've missed for each specific app. You don't realize how loud your phone is until you quiet it down. The red bubbles. The unread badges. The muscle memory of tapping into something just because it's there and it all adds up. Clearing my home screen created space. Literally. Visually. Mentally. It gave me a beat to ask myself: *Do I actually need to be doing this right now?* Most of the time, the answer was no.

Now, if I want to check something, I have to go looking for it. That tiny friction helps me break the autopilot cycle. It reminds me to be a little more present, a little more intentional, and a lot less reactive. My phone doesn't get to call the shots anymore. I decide when and why I open it. And when I do? It better be worth it.

Let your phone become a **tool of expansion**, not depletion.

I consider phones to be the binky in your pocket. They pacify us when life feels too loud or too dull. We use them to self-soothe, or when we need the next dopamine hit. There's no more boredom. No more idle moments that invite daydreaming. No more passing glances that spark conversation with strangers. We've replaced it all with tiny screens and we wonder why we feel disconnected. We scroll to feel better. We scroll to check out even if we're saying we're checking in. We scroll to avoid whatever feeling we're not ready to name. We scroll because silence feels dangerous. Because presence feels too raw. Because stillness forces us to hear what we've been avoiding. But healing doesn't live in the next notification. Healing lives in what we're willing to face without distraction.

And I get it. *I am no exception.* I'm flawed. I get caught in the spiral. This chapter is as much for me as it is for you. It serves as a reminder that we can be better. Family dinners are a **no phone zone** in our house. Because it's too easy to live parallel to the people we love most, without ever truly connecting.

There was a time I had to **break the addiction** entirely. I started charging my phone in a different room. Because I had trained myself to conveniently "not be able to sleep" around 2am and fall into the cycle. What started as checking the time turned into hours of doom scrolling. Morning would come too quickly, and I'd feel empty, exhausted, and I didn't even realize how deeply it had crept in.

Removing the phone from my room was one of the best things I could have done for myself. Actually, my kids aren't allowed to have their phones in their rooms either. Not because I don't trust them. But because I know how easy it is to fall into that pattern.

These days, I mostly check in on business. And as I continue to heal, I'm learning to use my phone more as a tool, not a lifeline. One thing that's helped? TikTok dates with my husband. It sounds silly, but they too, have been a game-changer. We'll set time aside to scroll together, laugh together, share videos that light us up. It's connection. It's joy. It's intentional.

The phone isn't the enemy, it's how we're using it.

***

I honestly think we've lost our creative outlets. There was a time when we doodled on napkins, wrote in journals, stared out the window and let thoughts drift. Now we grab our phones to fill the silence. Honestly, when was the last time you: Went to the bathroom without your phone? Stood in line at the store and just... stood there? Watched a full set of commercials? Sat in your car and watched the world go by? Again, I'm not here shaming you. And I'm not perfect. But I do think it's time we try, even just slightly, to be more intentional and more aware every chance we get.

I'm not going to sit here and tell you to stop using your phone. Let's be honest, most of us couldn't do it. And maybe we don't need to. But we **can** change what we're consuming. We can switch up the algorithm. We can shift the spiral. Want to heal? Start searching for reels that speak to your healing. Look for voices that remind you of your worth. Let your scroll become a soft place to land, not a place that sharpens your inner critic.

Want to get inspired to cook again? Start following creators who make it feel fun. Simple. Playful. Want to laugh more? Find the content that lights you up, not chaos. How much negativity have you allowed in your feed? The point is, you don't have to ditch your phone. But you do need to take back control of what you're feeding yourself. Because we are what we consume. And if we're constantly consuming fear, outrage, comparison, and overload, then of course we feel stuck. This isn't about quitting cold turkey. It's about injecting intention and awareness into the mindless moments. Let the scroll become intentional again. Not perfect. Not optimized. Just mindful. I know I'm starting to sound like a broken record here:)If your phone was a mirror for your mental health...what would it be showing you? Would you be proud of the thoughts it brings you? Or would you realize you've been feeding your mind the exact things you've been trying to heal from? You're not addicted to your phone. You're addicted to the feelings it triggers. Change the input. The output will follow. Welcome to your phone cleanse. Let it be the start of something different.

Reflection

What do you reach for your phone for most?

How do you feel after using it?

What content makes you feel energized? and what makes you feel small?

Where can you set new boundaries for yourself or your family?

- What creative outlet have you replaced with scrolling?

Affirmations

- I use my phone as a tool, not a crutch.

- I am allowed to be unavailable.

- I set boundaries around what I consume.

- My peace is more important than staying updated.

- I am mindful of what I feed my mind.

- I reconnect to the world beyond the screen.

And maybe the hardest part of shifting your phone habits...is realizing how often you were using it to **perform instead of connect.** We don't just scroll for entertainment. We scroll to feel seen. To feel something. To momentarily forget what we're not saying out loud.

And when we do post, sometimes it's not even real. It's curated vulnerability. Controlled intimacy. We share the breakdown, but only after we've processed it. We soften the truth until it sounds poetic enough to earn validation. But healing doesn't happen on a timeline. It doesn't always come with aesthetics. And it certainly doesn't require a hashtag. Because what most of us are really craving...isn't to be watched, but to be witnessed. And witnessing doesn't happen through a screen. It happens when we put the phone down, and show up.

Which brings us here: To the part where we talk about being *for real*, not just for show.

CHAPTER TWENTY

FOR REAL, NOT FOR SHOW

E arlier we were talking about alignment and how healing shows up not just in words but in action. How it lives behind the scenes in the quiet decisions no one claps for or even sees. But not every part of your healing is meant to be seen. Some parts are sacred. Some shifts are silent. Some truths don't belong on a stage.

That's where we're going now.

Let's talk about authenticity. Not the curated kind. Not the #healing caption next to a latte and a crystal. I'm talking about the kind of real that makes your throat close up. The kind that doesn't beg for likes. The kind that might never be witnessed by anyone but you (or the Universe). Or maybe just the mirror you've been avoiding. Because here's the truth: there's a big difference between being seen and being on display. A lot of us, especially women, have learned to perform vulnerability so well that even we start to believe it's the truth.

We cry pretty. We caption poetically. We open up just enough to look brave but not so much that we're actually at risk of being *known*. Because to be known? That's dangerous. That's exposure. That's the place someone could misunderstand you, or worse, *really see you*. I've done it. I've posted something that sounded honest but was really just a filtered version of my pain. I've crafted captions instead of making phone calls. I've written about healing while still chasing the validation that kept me stuck. I've performed strength while privately crumbling. And I'll tell you this: the performance might get applause, but it doesn't heal you. If anything, it keeps you disconnected from the very parts of yourself that actually *need* the love.

Being real doesn't always feel safe. And being loud about your healing doesn't always make it true. But here's what I've learned: You don't owe the internet your breakdowns. You don't have to turn your trauma into content. You don't need to spiritual-bypass your way into looking evolved. **Authenticity isn't for show. It's for you.** You can be honest and private. You can be tender and guarded. You can be deeply healing without posting a single thing about it. You don't need to explain

ALIGNING WITH

yourself to anyone. You don't need them to understand where you're coming from. They don't need to hear your side of the story. Some of your most powerful becoming will happen in silence. No audience. No affirmation. Just you, in the dark, figuring it the hell out. My biggest points of healing usually are shaped in my most disconnected times. Not the moments when everything's clicking and I'm full of clarity. Not when I'm journaling daily, meditating on schedule, or glowing in alignment. No, not at all.

My biggest healing doesn't happen when I feel connected. It happens when I feel lost. When I'm not posting constantly. When I'm disconnected from my routines. When I pull back from people I love, not out of spite, but survival. When the texts go unanswered and the dishes pile up. When I can't hear the Universe clearly, and my own intuition feels like it's on mute. That's when the real stuff starts bubbling up. The stuff I've been too busy (or too functional) to feel.

Because disconnection has a way of exposing what connection sometimes masks. When you're stripped of your distractions and patterns, the truth gets loud. And ugly. And honest. I've come to realize that those "off" seasons? The quiet, gritty, middle-of-the-night ones? They aren't a sign that I'm failing. They're proof I'm unraveling something that needs to go. Healing doesn't always feel like progress. Sometimes it looks like shutting down. Sometimes it sounds like silence. Sometimes it feels like failure. The version of me that breaks down in silence... well, she's not weak. She's the one who sets the next version of me free. So now, when I hit those disconnected stretches, I don't panic as much. I still feel the ache. I still wonder if I'm spiraling. But somewhere in the back of my soul, I know…This isn't the end. This is the molting. The cracking. The sacred dismembering before rebirth.

Healing isn't always about becoming someone new. Sometimes, it's about remembering who you were before the world told you to be less. And that remembering and rediscovery? It often starts in the dark because your story doesn't need a stage. It needs your presence. Ask yourself, Am I sharing this because it's real? Or because it's relatable? Is this *truth*? Or performance? What part of me am I still trying to protect by pretending I'm okay? Let me be clear, this isn't an attack on sharing. It's not about keeping everything private. It's about intention. It's about recognizing when your need to be witnessed has started to replace your need to be well. Sometimes, the most *authentic* thing you can do is *not* share it.

Let your growth take root where no one cheers you on for it. Let it be messy. Unphotogenic. Let it be yours. I'll be honest…here's the part no one likes to talk about, some of the people who *look* the most put together are barely hanging on. They've mastered the art of seeming okay. They've built brands out of looking healed. But when the door shuts, it's cold. It's silent. It's hollow. That's the cost of performance; you lose your connection to what's real. And real doesn't always look like a morning ritual. Sometimes it looks like crying in your car and not turning it into a reel. Sometimes it's choosing rest without announcing your "self-care." Sometimes it's saying no without softening it for other people's comfort. Real is choosing truth when no one is watching, or in direct contrast to their approval if they are. That's when it counts. That's when it's for *real*, not for show.

And if you're reading this, tired and a little bitter, wondering if any of this even works…You're not alone. You've read the books. You've journaled. You've said the mantras and lit the damn candles. And still, life hits hard. That's the moment right here, the one that matters. When belief starts to feel like pretending… this is where the *real* work begins. Because the magic isn't in the rituals. It's actually not even in the tools. It's in the *decision*. The shift from *"I hope this works"* to *"I've already decided it will."* You don't just trust the Universe when it says yes. You have to trust it when it says not yet. When it whispers wait. When it slams a door, you were begging to walk through. That's the difference between *looking* spiritual and actually *trusting*. So, if you're in that place, raw, restless, no filters left, I see you. And I'm with you.

Writing this chapter has felt like peeling off armor I didn't even know I was still wearing. I prefer to process things privately. To be composed. To make it make sense before I say it out loud. But this book is different for me. It's asking me to bring the truth even when it's jagged. So that's what I'm doing. Because I believe you don't become your highest self by staying small. You don't find your power in your polish. You find it in the moments where you almost didn't share. You find it when you walk away from what looked like a perfect life, because you knew it was a lie. Becoming her means being honest. This is your reminder, you don't owe anyone a performance of your becoming.

You just have to *keep becoming.*

Reflection:

- When was the last time you shared something that was *for real*...even if it wasn't pretty?

- Are there moments in your life where you were performing instead of being?

- What would it look like to share your story without needing applause?

- What part of your healing is just for you?

Affirmations:

- I don't need to be seen to be valid.

- My growth doesn't need to be pretty. It just needs to be mine.

- I choose truth over performance.

- I am safe to show up as I am...unfiltered, unpolished, and real.

- I don't perform my healing. I live it.

You can only sit with your truth for so long before it asks to move through you. Not just in thought, not just in stillness, but in motion. Because there comes a point where knowing isn't enough. You have to embody it. Live it. Let it shape your choices, your rhythm, your day.

After all the reflecting, unlearning, and feeling... the question becomes: **Now what?**

And the answer isn't always another journal entry or spiritual download. Sometimes, it's simpler than that.

Move.

Let your body lead when your mind feels stuck. Let momentum carry what meditation couldn't shift. Because movement clears the static and makes room for clarity.

This next chapter isn't about pushing harder. It's about trusting that your next step (even if it's messy) is the one that changes everything.

CHAPTER TWENTY-ONE

MOVEMENT IS THE MUSE (AND SOMETIMES THE MASK)

I get more done in the chaos of my life than I ever do in the stillness. Not because chaos is ideal but because it keeps me moving. And movement, not peace, is where my inspiration lives. Don't expect inspiration from stagnation. It's not coming. You're not going to wake up one day and feel suddenly "ready." You're not going to lay still long enough to birth a masterpiece. Rest has its role, but it's not the generator, it's the recharge.

If you're waiting for clarity to come find you, it won't. It meets you in motion. In messy action. In halfway ideas. In the middle of the damn kitchen floor while you're beckoning the kids to "please hurry" for the third time and also thinking of the next big thing. The muse shows up when you do. We've been fed this lie that we need perfect conditions to create, to build, to transform. But I've learned something truer: Chaos creates pressure. And pressure creates diamonds. You don't need more time. You need to stop trying to be graceful about it. You need to give yourself permission to be clumsy, loud, reckless, fiery. To make something ugly first, and then refine it. Stillness is sacred, but it's not a substitute for starting. If you're looking for inspiration, stop trying to manifest it from the couch. Get up. Shake things loose. Move your body. Take the step. Say the thing. It's not the peace that stirs your soul, it's the momentum.

Start where you are. Start while it's messy. Start in the chaos. Start, and the spark will follow.

This book has been going on two years in the making. Okay, not two "everyday" consistent years. I swear, the time that I get inspiration to write is when my life is in absolute fucking chaos. When I have literally no time to sit at a computer and get all of this out. It always seems to be inconvenient. Like right now, I am about to head to a session, but I get these moments of "must." This book has taught me patience. I am typically a "must finish everything as soon as possible" type of person. I will stay up for hours on end editing photos as to not leave them for the following day. The madness I get from leaving projects unfinished is painful. My brain won't stop. It's better for me just to complete it.

But this book? Haha, this book is everything but. It's "you have 5 minutes, go throw down those thoughts" or "you don't want to lose this, better scribble it down." The frustration I have to manage after getting into flow only to have to get up and move to the next thing on my to-do list? It's maddening. But I have learned so much about myself in these past few months. The progress I've made despite my schedule being absolutely bombarded... it's more than I ever expected. I have done more in the movement of the everyday than I have in the quiet days. It didn't make sense to me at first. But now I get it: every step closer is a step closer...even if there are steps back. We are still moving. Not stagnant. But if I'm being honest, I used to wear movement like armor. If I kept going, kept building, kept doing, I didn't have to sit with the parts of me that were unraveling. Stillness makes space for the questions I don't always want to answer. Am I doing enough? Am I enough? Chaos became the distraction that looked like drive. But eventually, I had to ask, am I thriving in the motion, or hiding in it?

***

A (not so) quick note:

Before we go any further, I need to name something that might already be stirring in you... Not all movement is medicine. Some of it is a disguise. A way to, you know, stay *ahead* of the stillness. A way to avoid the questions that inevitably rise up when things get quiet. We've been taught that hustle and motion equal progress, but let's be honest; sometimes that's just NOT the case.

Ask yourself:
"Am I moving toward something or away from something?"
"Does this action feel expansive, or tight in my chest?"
"What comes up for me when I pause?"

Movement that *heals* will ask for presence. Movement that *hides* will demand avoidance. You don't have to stop the motion, just check the intention behind it. Stillness isn't weakness. It's where truth has room to breathe. We just need to make sure we aren't filling our schedules to hide from our truths.

If you find yourself afraid of stillness because of what it might say back to you, GOOD. Listen. That's where the healing begins. But if you're not afraid of the stillness...if you're just stuck – if the lack of motion is hardening around you like concrete setting...that's not a weakness either. It's a signal. The longer you wait, the harder it is to chip your way out. But don't worry, you *can*. This is where you have to make your choices. This is where you have to see the glimmers. You just need to understand you're literally one choice away from breaking free.

✦ How Do You Know the Difference?

So how do you know if your movement is a disguise or the medicine?
How do you know when you need to move... and when you actually need to sit your ass down and *feel*?

It's simple. You ask. But not like a checklist. Not like a quiz with right or wrong answers. You ask like someone who's *ready to listen*...not just ready to be told.

Ask yourself:

- "If I stopped right now... what would come up?"

- "Am I afraid of the stillness, or am I just uncomfortable with the truth that might surface in it?"

- "Does this pace feel like freedom or pressure?"

- "If I stopped *doing* for a full day... would I still feel valuable?"

- "Am I using this action to build... or to avoid?"

Sit with the answers, even if they suck.

Here's the thing no one wants to say:
Sometimes movement *is* the medicine.
And sometimes it's the *numbing* agent.
The same tool can heal or hide...you don't know until you check the energy behind it.

If your motion feels frantic, tight, compulsive or like you'll unravel if you stop? That's not movement for growth. That's movement for *protection*. But if your movement feels aligned, even when it's messy or chaotic...if it leads to expansion, clarity, relief? That's your yes.

And if you're not sure? Try stopping for one full hour. Just one. Turn off the phone. Pause the scrolling. Step away from the to-do list. Get quiet enough to hear what bubbles up. If your body sighs in relief...that's your clue.
If your body tenses up and your brain gets loud, well...that's a clue too. You're not wrong for needing motion. You're not wrong for needing stillness. You just need to know which one is *calling you right now*.

And trust me: your body always knows.

***

As I've been writing this, at least in this current moment, I'm in the movement/motion side of things. But I want to be honest with where I'm at. What

152

it looks like, for me, so that maybe you are able to break down what it looks like for you. Hopefully it'll help you see where you're actually at.

I've had to put some things on the back burner. Weekly chats with friends most especially. But once they see that this was the reason, I honestly doubt they'll be surprised. As my soul sis would say, "Of course. This is just her new hunt." And she's right. I am in the ever-evolving pattern of finding something new to light me up. She is often my compass and reminder of rest. I can't wait for her to see this.

Clarity exists in movement. Action creates ripples. Stagnation only produces more stagnation, frustration, and irritation. When my schedule is wildly busy, I thrive. Truly. When I'm aligned, I thrive in chaos. When my schedule is stagnant, I struggle. I feel worthless. Pointless. I *have* to be working on a project.

But even as I thrive in momentum, I'm learning to recognize the cost. Sometimes it's presence. Sometimes it's laughter at dinner I missed because my brain was still chasing the next thing. My youngest said something off the cuff and everyone lost it, but I only caught the tail end. I was three feet away and still missed the moment. Sometimes it's the weight in my chest when I realize I've built a life I forget to feel. This isn't about guilt, it's about reclaiming intention. Because I don't want to be so busy becoming that I forget to *be*.

I nearly always fall into a state of depression when I'm stagnant. I know the signs. I start falling back into phone numbing. I lose my joy. I start craving something...anything.

But getting up and moving again? That's the real struggle. When I'm in that space, I can hardly function.

That's why we build tools.

Talking. Space. Awareness. The garage. The soccer field. The walk around the block even when you don't want to go. The laundry rotation. The dishes. Pumping up soccer balls. It's in the everyday chaos that ideas arrive. In my garage, there's an old amp next to my rocking chair. On top of it, a blue beat up notebook with half-written thoughts and ideas that come to me while we're sitting in there. It doesn't look like much, but it has been a lifeline. I don't call it journaling. It's definitely more...planning than anything. How do I level up? Where do I go from here? Okay, I suppose it *is* journaling.

My life revolves around movement. Not sitting (unless it's intentional). It's all about intention.

I expected this book to be written in the perfect space, where I had ample time to just sit and create. But it's not. Not at all. It's being okay with small progress. It's listening to only 10 minutes of your audiobook while you're on the way to pick up your kiddo from school. But if you do that every day? That 10 minutes turns into 50 minutes by the end of the week. And 100 after 2 weeks. Small progress adds up.

You just have to be honest about what you want. You can literally make anything happen. If I could bottle this energy, I don't think anyone would want it. It feels heavy and light all at once. It feels like frustration and inspiration. It tastes bitter and sweet. I feel panic in my bones yet ease in my brain. But that's the magic of movement. It doesn't promise comfort. It promises truth.

So if you're in the middle of the motion, overwhelmed, stretched thin, chasing clarity while juggling life, I see you. I am you. This chapter isn't asking you to slow down. It's asking you to listen in the noise. And if chaos isn't your muse? That's okay too. Your movement might look like quiet consistency. Like walking. Like baking. Like breath. Stillness can be movement too...if it's intentional. Because the muse doesn't need silence. She just needs a crack in the chaos to slip through. You don't have to wait for peace to start. You just have to decide it's worth beginning anyway.

And here's what ties it all together: movement doesn't just inspire. It alchemizes. When you sit still for *too* long, the thoughts pool. They start to sludge. They have nowhere to go, so they turn on you. They loop. They trap you in your own head.

But movement, any movement, gives that energy somewhere to flow. It creates space. It lets the fear and frustration breathe instead of fester. Even if the movement is messy. Even if it's angry. Even if it's just walking to the end of the driveway barefoot and putting your feet in the damn grass.

Some days you can't just think your way out. You have to move your way through. You're not weak for needing motion. You're not broken for thriving in chaos. You're a force of nature, and sometimes nature needs a storm before the stillness. So, here's the truth: if you're drowning in your thoughts, don't wait to feel ready. Fucking move. Even when it's hard. Even when you have nothing left.

Especially then. Movement will meet you where you are. It will carry the weight with you. It will remind you that you're still here. Still trying. Still becoming. And that's more than enough.

You don't need a full rewrite of your life. You just need small shifts that invite momentum.

Reflection

- Keep a "chaos notebook" (or Notes app) nearby. Don't wait for the perfect time to write it all out, just *jot the spark* when it shows up.

- Voice memo your thoughts while doing dishes, folding laundry, or driving. Don't edit. Just release.

- Ask: *What would 10 minutes look like today?*

- Track momentum instead of milestones. Write down what you *did*, not what you didn't finish.

- Pick a space, your garage, your car, the walk around the block.

- Play a specific playlist there. Move your body. Let it become your signal for ideas to flow. (Laying in bed signals your brain it's time for sleep - figure out a place that signals your brain it's time to release ideas)

- "What's one thing I could do for 5 minutes that moves this forward?"

- "Where have I been waiting for perfection when I could just take a step?"

- "What would I do if I wasn't trying to get it 'right' today?"

Affirmations
I don't need a perfect space. I just need space.

- I trust inspiration to meet me in motion.

- Small steps are still steps.

- I make magic in the middle of the mess.

- Momentum is medicine.

And here's what I've realized through all of this: Movement will get you unstuck. But surrender will set you free. You can move, create, push, and pivot; but if your hands are clenched tight around how it's *supposed* to go, you'll miss the path that's actually meant for you. Because sometimes, even when we're moving... we're still trying to control it all. The timeline. The outcome. The next step. The response. But life doesn't work like that. And the more I try to force it, the more I hear the whisper: "Loosen your grip." So let's talk about what happens when we stop white-knuckling our way forward...

This next chapter isn't about pushing harder. It's about trusting that your next step (even if it's messy) is the one that changes everything.

CHAPTER TWENTY-TWO

OPEN HANDS (CONTROL)

W ho doesn't try to control everything? We try to control the timing of things. The outcomes. The way things are *supposed* to unfold. But the truth is, most growth doesn't happen in the plan. It happens in the in-between. The stretch where we're trying to grow into something more... but haven't yet learned the lessons required to hold it. That's the space where surrender lives.

Surrender is where the real magic is. Releasing control is the ultimate level up. It's the most terrifying and liberating thing you can do, because it requires trust in something bigger than your checklist, your hustle, your logic. It asks you to believe that the Universe has eyes you don't. That it sees a version of your life that's so wildly aligned that if you could glimpse it, you'd stop trying to micromanage the one you're clinging to now.

I've tried to control so many things. How people see me. (Who hasn't, right?!) How clients perceive my work. How money shows up. How my kids move through the world. How and when "it all comes together." But if I'm being really honest, I wasn't just trying to control the outcomes, I was trying to hide. I thought that if I could keep everything held tightly in my hands, maybe I wouldn't be *found out*. That I wasn't as confident as I pretended. That I was second-guessing every decision. That underneath the illusion of "having my shit together," I was just trying to survive.

We wanted to be seen as successful, not envied, but safe from failure. Like we were making it. But the cost of keeping that illusion up? It was heavy. It meant hiding the mess. Swallowing the chaos. And holding shame over anything that looked like weakness. Somewhere along the way, I learned that exposing the messy, made you vulnerable. And honestly, "vulnerable" didn't feel safe.

Every time I white-knuckle something, the Universe gently pries my fingers off. Not because it's trying to break me. But because I'm holding onto the small version of something much bigger than I can see. Letting go isn't passive. It's one of the most courageous things you can do.

***

It was 2019, and we were in Denver for an academic camp for my oldest at DU. But really? That weekend was for me too. I had finally scheduled a one-on-one mentoring session with a photographer I deeply admired. And it scared the hell out of me. Not the photography part. The alone part. The being-seen part. Koko has always been by my side. We're a unit. We go to family photo sessions together, make decisions together, build together. But this? This I had to do on my own. And every part of me wanted to run.

Her house was tucked away like something from a movie, ivy climbing the white picket fence, mist hanging low in the air, flowers spilling over garden beds. It should've felt dreamy. I mean, it *was*...but I couldn't bask in the beauty. My body was tight. My hands were sweating. My brain wouldn't shut up.

"What am I doing here? You're not good enough. You're wasting her time."

She welcomed me warmly as I walked through the white picket fence. We turned the corner of the house, moved up the stairs and entered a beautifully put together sunroom. She told me to make myself at home and left to grab us drinks, while I sat on her beige couch feeling like I was about to pass out. My mind was running non-stop. I had my laughable portfolio, a series of 8x10 prints thrown together in a folder. We talked briefly and she asked for the folder. I didn't want to hand it over. I was embarrassed. I internally panicked as she looked through my portfolio in silence, then gently separated the images into two piles.

"This one," she said as she lifted up an image of my kids, "this is where you're connected. You shoot differently when you care. You see differently." I nodded, a lump in my throat, because she couldn't have possibly known they were my kids. "And this one," she said, holding a photo of my dear friends, "you know them intimately, don't you?" I did. But how could she see it? What was different about those photos? I still don't know for sure. But maybe... maybe it was because I wasn't performing. I wasn't trying to impress or prove or perfect. I was just *being*. Maybe I was more present. Perhaps more grounded. Open-hearted. And somehow, that translated.

Maybe it wasn't the subject that made the difference. Maybe it was me. My energy. My connection. The way I let down my guard just enough for the lens to catch what words couldn't.

That's the thing about intimacy; it softens the photograph. It lets it breathe. And she saw that. She felt it. That's when I started realizing this was going to be beneficial beyond what I could imagine. The Universe was speaking to me through her. Not just about photography. About everything. We talked more about my insecurity. My weaknesses. Then she asked about Koko. I told her everything. How he's always there. How I feel safer with him by my side. How he's my anchor.

She smiled kindly. "When you stop using your husband as a security blanket," she said, "you'll reach heights you didn't know were possible."

Oof.

It knocked the air out of me. I didn't like it. I didn't want it to be true. She didn't understand our story, our rhythm, our bond. But that night, I sat on the porch swing of our Airbnb and, as usual, unpacked everything from the day. I told Koko what she said. And instead of disagreeing, he just said, "She's probably right." He wasn't defensive or offended, because he already knew what I hadn't accepted yet: I wasn't clinging to him out of love. I was clinging to him out of control. He was my safe harbor, yes, but also my excuse to stay small. With hiding behind Koko, I didn't have to take full ownership. I didn't have to stand on my own two feet. I didn't have to be seen. He protected me from ever having to face my fears of potential criticisms or challenges.

And my goodness, I was *so afraid* of being seen. Because being seen is vulnerable. Being seen is scary. Being seen means someone might look too closely and realize

I didn't believe in myself at all. He was vibrant. Confident. Reassuring. The steady voice. The warm handshake. The one who told clients we had them covered, while I quietly hoped he was right. He believed in me completely. And I...couldn't yet.

I let him talk about the business. I let him carry the certainty. I stayed the silent artist, tucked in the background, nodding along but never fully stepping forward. Because if I failed, *I* would have to carry it. But if *we* failed? At least we'd have each other. There was comfort in the shared risk.

But just me? On my own? That felt like too much.

If it was mine, truly mine, then the rejection would be mine too. And I wasn't sure I could survive that. Criticism. Doubt. Exposure. I didn't think I had the spine to stand in it. So I hid behind his light and behind the story we told together. I didn't love myself enough yet to believe I was worthy of being in the spotlight, too.

***

Opening your hands doesn't mean letting everything go. It means loosening your grip on how it *has* to go. It means trusting that your worth is not tied to your timeline. That rejection might actually be redirection. That some doors close because the hallway is the real transformation. That miracles often show up dressed as messes. I used to pray like the Universe was a vending machine. Input enough effort, belief, or "right" action, and out comes the result. But now I know better. This isn't about force. This is about flow. This is about partnership.

I no longer believe in hustling my way into blessings. I believe in being *available* for them. Being open to them. And that means having space in my hands, and my heart, to receive what's mine. You can't receive with clenched fists. You can't hear your intuition when you're screaming instructions at the Universe.

Surrender doesn't look like weakness. It looks like saying "I don't know what's next... but I trust myself to figure it out." It's dropping the need to prove your worth. It's letting love in, even if it doesn't look like the version you had in your head. It's resting when your nervous system says "no more." It's following your gut even when your logic says, "this is insane."

Surrender is trust. Collapse is doubt. I've learned the difference the hard way.

Collapse is where you forget every tool that's helped you. Where you talk yourself out of healing. Where you search for evidence that nothing works, so of course, that's what you find.

Surrender is stillness with a heartbeat. It's a whisper that says, *"Keep tending the wall."* Even when it doesn't look like anything's growing. Even when the fog feels endless. Even when all you have to show for your effort is a watering can and cracked hands.

Actually, it's more like growing bamboo.

For years, bamboo shows nothing. No shoots. No sprouts. Nothing to prove that what you're doing is working. But underneath the surface, it's building something sacred...an intricate root system, strong enough to support explosive, unstoppable growth.

And then, when it's ready, *when it knows the foundation is strong enough*, it shoots up several feet in mere days. That's what surrender feels like. Like watering dirt while everyone around you is harvesting. Like being asked to trust that the miracle is already in motion, even when your eyes can't see proof yet. You wonder if you're behind. You wonder if you missed your window, but bamboo doesn't bloom on your schedule. It blooms when it's ready to hold the sky. You wonder if all this healing and hoping is just one long delay. But the truth is: you're not behind. You're becoming. (Are you tired of hearing that yet?)

Bamboo doesn't rush. It roots.

And maybe this isn't your season to bloom. Maybe it's your season to *anchor*. To deepen. To steady. To trust that something is building beneath you. And when it's ready? You won't be able to stop what's coming. It will rise *because you're ready to hold it.*

Our trip to Denver...I didn't know it at the time, but it was the prelude to my healing. I didn't fly home transformed, instead, I drove home cracked open. Confused. Tender. But also... different. That version of me didn't know she was starting a journey. But she was. The seed had been planted. Sometimes the spiral doesn't feel spiritual. Sometimes it feels like depression. Like self-doubt. Like old fears dressed in new clothing. And sometimes you have to sit in it, not because it's noble, but because you can't move until you've had enough of your own bullshit.

You don't always *choose* to sit in the underworld. Sometimes it pulls you under. But eventually, you remember: you've been here before. You've climbed out before. And you'll do it again. Because even the underworld grows roots. And even the darkest season has a moment when you unclench your fists. And whisper: Open hands. Open heart. Open path.

Reflection:

- Where in your life are you trying to micromanage the outcome?

- What would it feel like to stop gripping and start trusting?

- What's one area where you could practice opening your hands, just a little?

- When was the last time you surrendered control and something better than you expected happened?

Affirmation:

I trust that what's meant for me doesn't need to be forced. I release the need to control what's unfolding. I am open to being guided. I am safe to let go. I don't need all the answers to take the next step.

Sometimes it doesn't matter how aligned you are, how intentional you've been, how deeply you believe in healing, life still knocks the wind out of you. And when it does, most of us don't ask for help. Instead, we shrink or we isolate. We slap on a smile and keep showing up like everything's fine, even when it's not. Because we've been taught that holding it all together is strength. That falling apart makes us weak. That if we just push through hard enough, we'll find our way back. And we start living with open hands. But what if the breakdown isn't something to hide? What if it's the part that lets the light in? What if the very thing you're carrying right now... isn't meant to be carried alone?

CHAPTER TWENTY-THREE

THE WEIGHT OF CARRYING THINGS ALONE

W e think we have to do it all. Carry it all. Hold the house together, the calendar, the emotions, the needs, the unexpected. Be the glue, the anchor, the strength. We're taught that vulnerability is weakness and that carrying everything alone is a badge of honor.

And sure, maybe you do get stronger. But at what cost? Why do we do this to ourselves? Why do we insist on holding all the weight until we break? Most of the time, we don't even realize how heavy it's gotten. It's that slow layering. A little here. One more thing there.

A favor. A deadline. A fear. A secret. Until eventually, you can't hold it anymore. And you snap.

Not long ago, I found a lump in my breast. And I spiraled. It wasn't a dramatic spiral, at least not on the outside. I still showed up, still did the things, still smiled. But inside? I was unraveling. I didn't want to say anything to anyone. I didn't want to burden them. Didn't want to worry them if it ended up being "nothing." But it wasn't nothing. It was *something*, because it was happening to me. It was living in my body, taking up space in my mind, keeping me up at night. That's not nothing. And when we treat our fear like it's not valid, because we're afraid it might inconvenience someone else, we suffer silently. We convince ourselves that no one will understand. That our fear will be dismissed. That we have to hold it until we know the "outcome." But waiting alone is its own kind of torture.

I cried a lot that week. I kept thinking about what it would be like if I wasn't here. How my kids would remember me. What photos they'd have. What stories they'd carry. When we're faced with our mortality, even if it's just perceived, it wakes something up.

One night, while I was still waiting on results, my 8-year-old came in saying he didn't feel good. I hadn't been sleeping well, and I just fell into a deep sleep. I was exhausted. It was actually a struggle for me to get out of bed at that moment. I took him downstairs, got him some water, and sat with him on the bathroom floor. I was **so** tired. But then I thought: *What if this is the last time I get to take care of him like this?*

And suddenly, it wasn't a burden. It was a gift. A quiet, tender, unglamorous moment of motherhood, and I soaked it in. I quietly sobbed.

Eventually, I told a couple close friends. Not because I wanted to. But because they felt something was off. And when I told them, they didn't throw solutions at me. They didn't try to fix it or make it positive. They just sat with me. And that made it lighter. Not fixed. Not gone. But *lighter*. That's the power of letting someone help you carry it. And I'll be honest, allowing others in is hard for me, but I imagine I'm not the only one that feels this way.

To be painfully honest, I'm guilty of the opposite. I throw out positivity like confetti. I genuinely believe the Universe is *for* us. That everything is working in our favor. Even when things feel like they're falling apart, I know in my bones that it's a redirection. I was supposed to find this as a reset and a lesson. I even annoy myself.

I understand that sometimes people don't need the spiritual spin. They need the truth to sit still. To be seen. To be felt. They need someone to stay *with* them in it, not around it. I've learned that there's a time for hope, and there's a time for stillness. And knowing the difference? That's where true connection happens.

Let's talk about it. We say it all the time: *"holding space."* But what does that actually mean? Especially when the person hurting is someone you love?

Holding space is the choice to witness someone's pain without trying to fix it. It's being present, not powerful. It's being *with* someone, not over them. It looks like letting them cry without rushing them to calm down. Saying, "That makes sense," instead of "At least it's not worse." Asking, "Do you want advice, or do you want me to just sit with you?" Staying in the room, even when the conversation is messy. It's asking questions, but not with a point you're trying to prove. I think of it more like, asking questions so they can unwrap the things that are tangled in their minds.

It's not offering silver linings. It's not telling your own version of the story. It's not wrapping their pain in a pretty bow.

Holding space means choosing to *feel with*, not *fix for*.

And yes, it's harder when it's someone you love. Because their pain hurts you, too. Because you want to make it go away. Because you hate feeling helpless.

But you're not helpless. You're *there*. And that's the most powerful thing you can do.

If I'm honest, this past year has been a wrecking ball. This is where I get really vulnerable (again). Where I lay some things out that I think probably *shouldn't* be brought up. Where shame is the ever-present feeling and the aftermath is something we are still struggling with.

My husband's sister was charged with murder. Even now, that sentence doesn't feel real. Like I'm borrowing someone else's nightmare. It's important to say this gently and clearly: this chapter isn't about the details of that case or meant to minimize the tragedy. A life was lost. Families were shattered. There is a victim. There are so many victims.

What I'm writing about is what happens after the sirens fade. The quiet devastation. The long, painful unraveling of a family trying to carry what can't be carried alone. What I didn't expect was how it opened my eyes to a kind of grief we don't often talk about, the grief of the family on the other side of a horrific crime. The ones related to the person who committed the unthinkable. You don't see a lot of compassion for them. And honestly, I didn't understand it either. Not until it became our reality.

Because we weren't just devastated. We were *furious*. It was anger at the choices made. At the violence committed. At the life that was taken. And alongside that anger was a deep confusion, where do we fit in this story?

My husband was grieving the sister he still had, while mourning the version of her he lost.

We didn't ask to be part of this. But here we were. Mourning the person we thought we knew. Grieving a version of family we'd lost. And still holding sorrow for the life that was taken.

That's a heavy, messy place to be. And there's no map for how to grieve someone you still love while condemning what they've done. There's no script for being the family left behind on the other side of the crime scene tape.

It completely broke Koko.

Then his favorite uncle died. Another loss. Another rock on the pile. But this one was different. This one *hurt*. He wasn't just an uncle; he was one of those rare souls who made people feel seen the second they entered a room. The kind of man who had a story for every moment and laughter that felt like home. Koko admired him fiercely. His steadiness. His warmth. His quiet way of being a lighthouse without ever needing the spotlight.

But he was also loud in the best kind of way. A big personality, easily my favorite person in Koko's family. Vibrant. Full of love. The kind of man who walked into a room grinning ear to ear, already halfway through a joke. He loved riling up kids and dogs. Gave the best hugs. Made the loudest laughs feel safe. He was silly and wholehearted and exactly the kind of genuine human the world needs more of, and now there's one less.

He was the person Koko could talk to without filtering anything. There was never any judgment. No pressure. Just presence.

And when he passed, it felt like one of the last safe places in the world went quiet. Especially following the loss of his beloved grandfather in 2023 that he still struggles with. This wasn't just another loss. This was a *bright spot* going out. A part of his foundation crumbling. I watched the grief settle in like fog. (And maybe you've felt that too. The part of you that goes missing when someone you love disappears.) And I watched him start to slip. Quietly. Slowly. He wasn't himself. And I worried: *Am I missing the signs? Is he okay?*

I knew the answer. I could feel it.

So, I reached out to one of my closest friends and asked for help from her network. Not therapy, not in the clinical sense, because that system had failed him in the past, and I knew he wouldn't be open to it. But healing. Connection. Support. And she responded with something that hit me hard: *"I'm proud of you for reaching out."*

Because reaching out *is* brave, sweetheart.

It's easy to pretend you can carry it all. But asking for help? We're taught its weakness. That's **not** weakness though, it's wisdom.

That same morning, I broke down. The fear, the exhaustion, the pressure, it cracked me open. But when you're breaking, you can't always feel strong. You just feel alone. Tired. Weak. Pathetic.

But you're not. You're none of those things. You're just carrying too much.

If you're carrying something heavy, say something. Even if you don't know how. Even if you're scared it's "nothing." Even if you've convinced yourself no one will understand. *Someone will.*

And even if they can't take it away, they can sit with you in it. You don't have to hold the weight of the world alone. You were never meant to. Koko started the alternative, holistic style therapy. Only now, nearly 7 months later, and nearly 2 months into healing is he starting to come back to life. We have to take a stand for those we care about. We have to reach out. We have to be honest about where we're at.

***

Because when you *do* carry it alone, when you push through without pause, without help, without release, <u>your body keeps score</u>. Your energy does, too. Because energy is an investment. Every thought, every mood, every interaction is a deposit...or a withdrawal. And like any investment, the return multiplies, sometimes quietly, sometimes massively. The Universe doesn't just receive your energy; it compounds it. What you send out echoes back.

Here's the kicker: just like good energy pays dividends, unprocessed emotion and heavy energy can create *debt*. And that debt shows up in ways we don't always recognize.

It looks like snapping at your kids over nothing. It looks like avoiding your inbox or ghosting your friends. It looks like laying in bed, not tired, but *numb*. It feels like disconnection, from others, from joy, from *yourself*. We start thinking we're the problem. That we're lazy. Unmotivated. Overly sensitive. But really? We're just in energetic overdraft. And that's not a flaw. That's a sign. A signal. A reminder to reconnect. To offload. To breathe. It's those grey days that start creeping in and compounding.

We carry things that don't belong to us. We carry fear we never speak aloud. We carry each other, quietly, often clumsily; but the truth is: we're not meant to carry *everything* alone. You don't have to earn the right to be supported. You don't have to collapse in order to be held.

You're allowed to say, *"This is too heavy."* You're allowed to say, *"I'm not okay."* You're allowed to ask someone to sit in the dark with you, even if there's no fix. Because sometimes the most powerful thing we can do for each other isn't to make it lighter. It's to make it *shared*. And that, too, is healing.

When you're just trying to survive, you forget to live. You forget the tiny moments that make a life; a lunch packed with love, a shared laugh before school, the morning playlist that used to feel like magic. You stop showing up with joy because joy feels like a luxury you don't deserve.

But it's not. It's the fuel. It's the spark. It's the reason you started this life in the first place.

Somewhere along the way, we both got tired. Survival kicked in and numbness took over. The mornings got heavy. No one left the house energized. No one laughed like we used to. And I realized something... I forgot to be the character I used to play in our mornings. The silly one. The light bringer. The "this is *still meaningful*, even when it's chaos" one.

So now? We set intentions. Not to be perfect. But to be *present*. We treat our joy like a recharging station. We let breakdowns be breakthroughs. We hold space for each other when life is falling apart. We seek out therapy, whether it's clinical or holistic. We share with our friends without feeling like a burden. We remember that sometimes, to launch back to the top, you have to push off the bottom.

And we say we *get to*, because even this, this messy morning moment, is a gift.

Reflection

- What are you currently carrying that no one knows about?

- Who in your life could you practice being vulnerable with?

- Have you ever tried to fix someone's pain instead of sitting with it?

- What does holding space look like for you?

Affirmation

I am worthy of support. I don't have to carry this alone. My vulnerability is not a burden; *it's a bridge to connection*.

So now, here's what we're remembering:

- **Set intentions.** Even if it's as small as "I will move through today with lightness."

- **Use tools.** Tiny reminders, maybe a note in your pocket, a bracelet, a song...all of these can be lifelines back to alignment.

- **Choose presence.** Not performance. Not politeness. Real, honest, "this is what I need" kind of presence.

- **Let the Universe experience joy through you again.** Laugh. Play. Dance. Coach the game like it's about the kids' hearts, not the scoreboard. Show up because you *want* to - not because you *have* to.

Because your emotional currency is important. Grace should never cost you your truth. And because love, *real* love, holds space for all of it.

Chapter Twenty-Four

The Day I Almost Quit

I'm supposed to be the one who gets us back on track. That's the unspoken agreement, right? I'm the one who recalibrates the energy. The one who dreams big, pulls the pieces together, and brings the light back when it's gone. But today? I don't want to be the light. I don't even want to be visible. I want to scream into a pillow and not have to justify why I'm tired.

There's been a cloud over this house for months. A heaviness that's soaked into the walls. Into Koko. Into me. At first, I thought it would lift. That it was just a season. That we'd bounce back. But instead, I've felt myself sinking in it, wallowing with him, as Koko put it. And maybe I am. But I'm also surviving and that shouldn't have to be defended.

Because here's what no one tells you about being "the strong one"…Eventually, you run out of rope too. And there's no one there to throw it back to you. I know the bank account is a flashing warning light. I know my business has dipped. But I also know this, I can't force creativity. I can't fake energy. I can't book sessions while hiding the fact that I feel like *I'm the one who needs saving right now.*

And what do you do when the thing you built to empower others starts to feel like another place you have to perform? And when you're the one people come to for light, what happens when you go dark?

You almost quit. You consider burning it all down. Not out of drama, but out of desperation.

But then, there's this *tiny whisper* under all the noise. Not loud. Not glowing. Just quiet enough to make you pause. It says, "You've felt like this before and you made it through. You can do hard things but you don't have to do them all at once." And I remember this moment isn't the ending. This isn't the chapter they quote. This is the part most people skip over when they talk about *healing*. It's not glamorous. It's not graceful. It's gritty and sad and angry and scared all at once.

But it's real. And maybe that's what someone else needs more than a perfect comeback story.

Maybe what saves us isn't pretending we've risen, it's admitting that we almost didn't.

I'm not out of it.

If you're reading this hoping for a clean resolution, a motivational one-liner, a breakthrough that wraps it all up in a pretty little bow, this isn't that part. This is the part where I tell you I'm *still here,* in it. In the thick of it. In the pit. Not metaphorically. *Literally.*

Today, I feel hopeless. Like there's no light. Like I can't find the tools. Like the pages I wrote before (tools I believe were handed to me by the Universe for others) can't even reach me now. I read my own words trying to "snap out of it." I tried to listen like I was the reader instead of the writer. But nothing's snapping. Nothing's unlocking. I'm still here. Have you felt that too? The disorienting distance between what you know and what you can feel?

And I don't want to keep being the black cloud. I don't want to be the one who always needs help. So I've stopped reaching out. Not because I don't love my people, but because I can't keep showing up soaked in grief and guilt and expect them not to flinch.

I won't let myself cry. Because what would that even *do*? The dishes still need to be washed. The sessions still need to be booked. The family still needs to be fed. There's no time for tears. There's no space for softness. There's only survival.

And I'm tired of surviving.

I'm consumed by the life I *could* be living. The momentum I *should* have. The potential that hangs just out of reach, taunting me. Like a mirror showing me everything I'm not living up to. And it hurts. It hurts to want something so deeply and feel like I can't get there. Like I've lost the map.

And here's what I really want to say, what most people don't, I've hit "rock bottom" so many times, I'm starting to think the floor keeps falling out beneath it. I didn't know there were *layers* to rock bottom. But here we are.

So what now? Where do we go from here?

I don't have the answer yet. But I *know* this... Even in this moment, this messy, painful, soul-wrecking moment, there is still something sacred happening. I believe the tools are still here, even if they feel out of reach. I believe the Universe still has me, even if I can't feel it. I believe I am still the vessel, even if I feel cracked open and empty.

So maybe that's the next tool. Let the tool be truth. Not pretending. Not fixing. Just *telling the truth* of where you are. "I am in it. I feel lost. I feel ashamed. I feel like nothing is working. And I am still here." That's the tool. That's the medicine. Maybe that's how we start climbing, by admitting we can't climb yet. By letting the page hold what the body can't. By writing instead of running. By staying instead of escaping.

Tears silently slide down my cheeks. Koko is sitting across from me but doesn't dare acknowledge it. He knows I'm processing.

I don't draw attention to it. I don't shame myself for it, for once. I just let it be. I'm not crying so much as silently releasing. There's no sobbing. There's just surrender to these feelings. Surrender that I might have to sit here for a while. Surrender that I have to stop trying to force it. That I just need time. Fuck. How much more time can I possibly give? If I'm honest, I'm craving time at the ocean, but I know that's a tall order right now. So, naturally, I find myself needing to be in the forest. My feet need to be in a stream. I need to be enveloped by trees and a soft breeze. I need to reconnect. I am at my lowest low. My biggest disconnect. I've been scrambling to hold on. And now, I feel like in some ways, I'm giving up.

Does surrender feel like giving up? Is this surrender...or am I giving up? What's the line between trust and retreat? What is the difference of intention there?

Giving up, I suppose, means you no longer care. Surrendering is trusting the Universe.

Even as this flows out of me, I'm frustrated. Is it the same? Trusting the Universe while we're in the messy middle, in rock bottom, feels impossible. I'm even annoyed at myself, because my beliefs still nudge me. Over and over.

"This is happening for us."

We can't see why yet, but it is. Man, I really can be annoying. But maybe that voice (the one that still believes) isn't here to fix it. Maybe she's here to keep me from disappearing completely. And it's not like this is some tragic end. It's not like I have "real" shit to be agonizing over. I'm healthy. My family is healthy. I'm lucky in so many ways. It's just my mind's bullshit. Being burnt out. Letting people down. Letting my family down.

I feel like I keep hearing a whisper from the Universe:

"Keep going."

And I do. I try to.

But how many more days can I show up as half (or less) of myself? I've been trying to get back into the rhythm of *how do I be of service to the Universe?* But man, that's a tall freakin' order. How can I be of service to the Universe if I can't even be of service to myself? I believe that if we are of service to the Universe, the Universe balances it. Fully. Completely.

So is it because I'm not holding up my end of the bargain?

Am I so lost that I can't arrive for it? How do I snap out of it?

I wish I had the answers for you from this space. So let's just sit in it together. Let's say the things out loud - the shame, the frustration, the ache of wasted potential, the exhaustion from carrying everyone's "bounce back" expectations like they're gospel. Let's be mad at ourselves for not being further along. Let's be annoyed at how much we still *believe,* even while we're questioning everything.

But let's also decide, together, to give ourselves grace. Let's begrudgingly get out into nature, even if it's with puffy eyes and tangled hair and a heart that still feels heavy. Let's go find the stream. Let the trees hold what we can't. Let the breeze remind us what movement feels like again.

There's always a moment in the year, maybe even in the cosmos, where the Universe pulls the rug again. Where old wounds get triggered and new ones show up in their clothes. Where everything you thought you healed comes back just to ask, *"Are you different now? Are you really?"* It feels like a test. Not of strength. But of **trust.** And maybe this moment, this pit, isn't a punishment. Maybe it's a slow-burning truth.

Okay, fine.

Let's burn down the hurt. Not with rage, but with release. Let it smolder, not just the pain, but the belief that I always have to be the one holding it all together. Let the fire eat that part. Let it clear a space where my highest self can finally *breathe.*

Because even here, in the lowest of lows, when nothing feels good, when I'm numb and raging and tired all at once, and even though I've played with the idea, I haven't given up.

Not really. Even at rock bottom, I'm still listening. Still reaching for something, even if it's just a breath. Even if it's just a moment of stillness that doesn't ache. And maybe I don't need to scream to be heard. Maybe I just need to stop lying about how heavy it's been. How much I've been carrying. How long I've been pretending it was fine.

Maybe that's the loudest truth of all, not the resilience or the bounce back. Just the moment you admit you're in the thick of it, and you *still* believe you were made for more than this. Not in a loud, conquering way. But in a quiet, stubborn way. The kind that acknowledges, *"I don't have to prove it to anyone to make it true."*

Maybe... that's enough. Maybe that's where we begin again. Let's choose ourselves, not because it's easy. But because even in the lowest low, some part of us still insists we keep going. Let's not be silent anymore. Let's not rush past this one. Let's not skip ahead to the triumph or pretend we're ready to rise. Let's just sit here for a second. In the quiet. In the ache. In the truth.

You made it through the chapter, maybe with tears sliding down your cheeks, like me. Maybe with your jaw clenched. Maybe with nothing left to feel at all.

However you arrived here: *you're still here.* And that matters. This isn't a space for perfect answers. This is a space to echo back whatever's still ricocheting inside you.

Reflection:

- Where are you right now—*emotionally, energetically, spiritually*?

- Is there something you've been silently carrying that you're ready to name here?

- What part of this chapter cracked something open for you?

- What version of "rock bottom" are you trying to climb out of?

- What do you need to forgive yourself for right now, even if just a little?

- How do you define the difference between giving up and surrendering?

- What would it mean to stop trying to fix it, and instead just *feel* it?

- What is your ocean? What is your forest? Your stream? What is the place that could hold you today?

AFFIRMATIONS:

I don't have to be okay to be healing. I can hate this part of the process and still honor it. My softness is not weakness. My survival is necessary. I am allowed to pause before I rise. Even in the pit, I am still connected to something bigger.

Burn It: A Sacred Release Ritual

A first-class delivery to the Universe. Some words were never meant to stay on the page. Some wounds don't want to be healed, they want to be witnessed, then set free. This is your space for the messy. The heavy. The unspeakable. Write it all. The anger. The resentment. The exhaustion. Say what you've been afraid to say. *Let it be ugly.* Then tear the page out. Take it outside and burn it.

Watch the fire dance. Watch the flames curl around your pain like they understand it. See the smoke lift your truth. Let it rise. This is not destruction. This is transmutation. This is your message to the Universe, *first-class delivery, no return address.*

"This is no longer mine to carry. I release it with fire. I trust that what returns will be lighter, truer, and mine."

& Please do this safely. Use a fireproof bowl or outdoor space. Have water nearby. Honor the flame.

CHAPTER TWENTY-FIVE

YOU'RE NOT TOO MUCH

B y the time you reach this page, you've likely seen a pattern. We hold so much. We hold our dreams in one hand and our doubt in the other. We carry other people's emotions while barely managing our own. We shrink ourselves to avoid rocking the boat, while quietly wondering if anyone ever sees us fully. And through it all, we try to stay kind, to stay soft, and to stay us.

But here's what we're never really taught: Not everyone is built to meet you where you are. And that doesn't make them bad. That doesn't make you wrong. It just means you're wired differently.

Some of us are playing the long game of healing. Some are playing the short game of survival. We're using different rules, different clocks, different definitions of what "winning" even means. Some are building bridges in every conversation. Others don't even recognize there's a bridge being offered.

You show up thinking: Let's work through this. Let's hold space. Let's connect. They show up thinking: How do I defend myself? How do I win this? How do I stay safe?

You bring your heart. They bring armor. And you end up walking away thinking you messed it up.

I've left so many conversations wondering if I was the problem. Sitting in the car, replaying every word I said. Wondering if I was too emotional. Too intense. Too much. What about you? Maybe you've also replayed the conversation in your head until it bruised.

But I wasn't the one trying to win, I was trying to connect. And there's a difference. Let me say this clearly: You are not too much. Not too soft. Not broken for wanting more than surface-level everything. You're just playing a different game than the people who move through life trying to collect more, feel less, and avoid discomfort at all costs. When you choose to live open-hearted, you will lose people. People who need you to stay small so they don't feel threatened. People who misunderstand your boundaries as rejection. People who were never meant to walk this road with you.

That hurts. But it also frees you. Because with every person you lose, you become more of yourself. You start choosing truth over politeness. Alignment over approval. Integrity over fitting in. You start understanding this...

Authenticity will cost you something. But inauthenticity costs you everything.

And here's the part that hits hardest: We want to believe that if we lead with love, people will mirror it back. But not everyone knows how to do that.

Some never had safe places to land. Some never learned to process instead of react. Some never saw vulnerability modeled, so it feels like danger to them. They may not have the emotional tools you've worked so hard to build. So when you speak gently, they hear weakness. When you set boundaries, they hear betrayal. When you grow, they hear you leaving. But I really need you to feel this. Their projection is not your problem. Your job was never to contort yourself into a version they could understand.

Let this be the chapter where you stop trying to earn worthiness. Let this be the chapter where you stop blaming yourself for other people's discomfort. Let this be the chapter where you forgive yourself for softening your voice, shrinking your dreams, and dimming your joy just to stay digestible. Because the truth is, you don't need to be palatable. You were born to be real. And the people who are meant for you? They won't flinch at your bigness. They won't punish your boundaries. They won't confuse your kindness for weakness. They'll meet you in the middle of your journey and stay.

So if no one's told you lately: You're not imagining it. This life is heavy. But you are strong. And you don't have to carry it alone. Some people will meet you there. Some people are playing for connection. Some people are learning to build bridges, too. You are not the only one. And if you forget everything else in this book, remember this: Success isn't about who claps for you. It's about who you become when you stop hiding. You are allowed to be loud. To be soft. To pivot. To cry. To laugh. To be too much for the wrong people and just right for yourself.

You don't need permission to be who you are. This chapter isn't asking you to be louder. It's asking you to be truer.

Say it out loud if you need to: I am not here to be understood by everyone. I am not here to keep shrinking to fit. I am already enough, even unpolished, even becoming, even now.

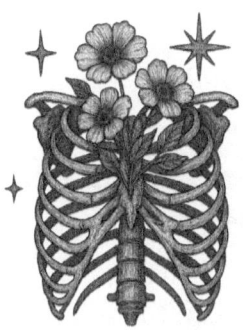

My Soul's Assignment

I didn't mean to become this person. I didn't set out to be introspective, or wise, or a mirror. I was just... left alone. Not metaphorically. Literally. No TV. No radio. No distractions. Just me, my breath, and the thoughts that wouldn't let up. Silence with my thoughts became my origin story. It became the first place I ever heard myself. And even then, I didn't fully believe her.

I don't always feel the joy. I don't always let the wins land. I don't always *believe* that what I'm doing is changing people's lives. And maybe that's part of the curse. The artist's curse. Not the suffering. Not the overthinking. But the **constant reaching**. The *what's next*. The refusal to sit too long in applause because the mission isn't done. You don't get to rest on one breakthrough when you know the world is still full of women breaking quietly. So I keep going. Not because I'm addicted to effort, but because I know what's at stake. Because I've lived in that place where no one came to check on you. And I promised I'd never leave another woman there. We don't deserve to be unheard or silenced.

One night after I got a message from a client explaining that the session was everything her soul needed and more, I felt like she was giving *me* too much credit. I just hold space, she was the one taking the journey. Koko told me, "You change people's lives like it's normal. You brush it off like it's not a big deal. But it's not normal. Most people never do that. And the fact that you don't even see it—that's part of your magic."

That's when it hit me.

The world doesn't know what to do with women who don't perform. Who don't compromise. Who don't sell their soul for a paycheck and call it success. The world is not built to honor women like us.

So we learn to doubt ourselves and to soften our truth. We learn to apologize when the room gets quiet. And I did that. For years.

But here's what I know now:

Most people aren't avoiding their purpose. They're just avoiding discomfort. The kind that comes when you stop people-pleasing. When you speak without qualifying your truth. When you name your value without blinking. It's terrifying to lean into that kind of boldness. But it's also liberating and completely misunderstood.

Because the systems we live in are *designed* to reward quiet compliance. To teach us that we are only as valuable as the work we can provide. And that self-worth should be measured in deliverables.

So no wonder it sounds strange when I say: You don't have to settle. You don't have to trade your soul for stability. You don't have to apologize for not fitting the mold.

That's why this book exists. Not to teach you something new. But to remind you of what you've always known but couldn't name. I didn't get this insight from a podcast. I didn't learn to "coach" myself through it. I *sat in it*. I lived in the silence. I conversed with every version of me. And maybe that's why my message lands the way it does...because it isn't theory. It's not rebranded self-help. It's not a filtered affirmation with good lighting.

It's *earned*. Earned in the silence. Earned in the chaos. Earned in the moments no one clapped, no one saw, no one helped me up.

So now I speak a bit unfiltered. I speak unsoftened. I am not a fan of honeyed words. I want to know the truth. And I'm still learning to be unapologetic. And I remind myself, when I feel the urge to shrink or second-guess:

Let that be enough. Let this moment, this message, this knowing...be enough. You don't have to convince them. You don't have to overperform. You don't have to explain your price, your posture, your power. You just have to embody it.

So if you're reading this and if you've ever felt like maybe you're not "doing enough"... Like you need another degree, another milestone, another round of proof before you're allowed to take up space...I'm here to say:

Let that be enough. Your truth. Your timing. Your voice. Let that be enough.

Because it already is.

CHAPTER TWENTY-SIX

THE BOOK IS WRITING US BACK

I swear the Universe has a sense of humor. Because some days, it feels like the only reason we're going through all this shit is so the book writes better. Like, maybe the Universe looked at our life and said, *"Oh, you wanna write about healing and success and showing up through the mess? Cool. Let me give you some new material."*

And we *got* the material.

Breakdowns, burnout, unspoken tension, heavy mornings, lightless nights. But also, the breadcrumbs back to ourselves. Epiphanies, laughter in the swing set shadows, goosebumps at the perfect sentence, yellow birds as messengers of brighter days. The highs and the lows are carving the story, and I'm starting to believe that maybe we're not just writing the book...**the book is writing us back.**

This season is not punishment. It's pressure. Pressure that turns straw into gold. Pain into prose. Doubt into deeper knowing. Like the tormented artist or the mythic loom that spins from nothing but hay, we're spinning heartache into something helpful.

And you know what? We would do it again. Not because we love the hurt, but because we love the clarity that follows. The *I see it now.* The *we made it anyway.*

The *we are the proof.* Every page was a mirror. Every chapter a breadcrumb. Every sentence pulled me closer to the version of myself I hadn't fully met yet.

And if you've made it this far, I bet the same is true for you.

Because here's the thing: This isn't a book you just *read*. It's a book you *become*. You didn't just underline the good parts; you felt them in your chest. You didn't just highlight the tools; you saw your own habits in between the lines. You didn't just read the messy middle, you remembered that you're not alone in yours. This wasn't (or isn't) just a self-help journey. It's a recalibration. We're not stuck anymore, we're sculpting. Taking heavy energy and reshaping it into truth. Into tools. Into light.

If you're hitting rock bottom, just know, it's the bounce from the bottom of the pool. It's seeing the light draw nearer as you move toward the surface. It's the spring that comes after the weight. It's the shift. I feel it. I know it.

This is it. **This is the part where we start living again.** And now? Now you don't go back. Now you don't get to un-know what's been revealed. Now you don't get to pretend your voice doesn't matter, or that your softness isn't strength, or that your dreams are too big.

Because now you've seen it. Not just what's possible, but what's *already here*. Let this be the moment you stop waiting for proof. Let this be the moment you trust what you've already become. You weren't supposed to stay hidden forever. You were supposed to *outgrow* the spaces that no longer felt like home. You were supposed to *bump against the edges* of your old stories until they cracked. You were supposed to evolve.

And you did.

You said no when it would've been easier to say yes. You showed up on the grey days. You got honest about your patterns. You stopped believing your own bullshit. You stopped performing healing and started actually healing. And maybe you're not where you want to be yet. But now, you know where you're not willing to go back to.

This book means the world to me. It is so many thoughts that have been bouncing around...a space, finally a space, where they can rest. It's conversations from my studio that I hear over and over, conversations that are life changing. It's all the ideas that have helped shape and change my life. It's tools that are a part of my every day. This book is a living journal of becoming. And I'm so proud of it.

If you're scared, good. Being scared is your ego. It's the confirmation of change. It's the sign you've been waiting for. If you're scared, that's the surest sign that you are on the right path. Your ego is trying to keep you safe. It doesn't like unfamiliar territory. So let's ask: What are you so afraid of? Let's start there.

Because once you name it, it loses its power. And once you face it, you gain yours.

I became someone my past self desperately needed. Someone who trusts her voice. Someone who doesn't need everyone's approval. Someone who can hold space without abandoning herself. The self-doubt and limiting beliefs used to live rent-free in my mind. My family is loving, but cautious. Supportive in their way but scared of the unknowns I was chasing. They struggled with a lot of my choices. And so the supportive voices I needed weren't always the loudest. But now? Now I am that voice for myself. And maybe, for you too.

So, what now? Now...you build. You choose. You live the life that used to feel out of reach. You let the tools live on your bathroom mirror, in your playlist, in the way you answer your phone. You let your energy, your joy, your presence become your loudest message. You let people misunderstand you and stay soft anyway. You let the messy middle be sacred instead of shameful.

You let your story stay open. Because the truth is: The Universe didn't just call you to read this book. It called you to write the next chapter. Not on paper. But with your life.

Reflection:

When you look at who you were when you started this book...What's changed? What did you stop carrying? What did you finally give yourself permission to want? What part of you has come home.

Affirmation

I am not the same person who opened this book. I am more honest. More whole. More awake. I am not waiting for permission. I'm already in motion. The story isn't over. But the hiding? That part IS over.

Soul Tools

Here's what I come back to when I forget that the story still has more chapters:

- **When it feels like everything is falling apart, ask:** *Is this the scene that makes the story worth telling?*

- **Reframe the breakdown:** This is the moment before the bounce. The spring only works if you have something solid to push off from.

- **Give the pain a purpose:** Journal prompt: *What's one thing I'm experiencing right now that might be turning me into a better version of myself?*

- **Live like the book is watching:** Ask: *If I were reading this version of me in a chapter, what would I want her to do next?*

CHAPTER TWENTY-SEVEN

A NOTE FROM THE OTHER SIDE

T his book started in the thick of it. Most of the time, I didn't even know what I was writing toward...I just knew I wasn't willing to hide anymore. I poured pieces of myself onto these pages while still mid-mess, mid-healing, mid-question.

Now, months later, as I revisit these chapters and reread my own words, I can feel the space that's been created. Not because life is "fixed," but because I stopped trying to perfect the mess before writing it down.

Some of what I wrote came from heartbreak. Some from hope. And now, I can tell you, not as a teacher, but as someone who's still in it: the tools work. Maybe not instantly. Maybe not all at once. But slowly, steadily, and undeniably... they work.

Most of these tools evolved. Some I had to learn the hard way. Some showed up when I wasn't even looking. And now? They're tucked away in my back pocket for when I need them. I still discover new ones. I still outgrow old ones. I've changed. I'm still changing. And that's the whole point, isn't it?

This chapter isn't a tidy bow. It's a conversation across time. A few reflections from the other side of things that once felt all-consuming. A chance to walk you back through the middle—with fresh eyes, deeper breath, and more clarity than I had when I first wrote it down.

Chapters 2 & 5:

We Don't Do That Anymore + What Am I Fighting For?

Then: "Not everything deserves a front-row seat in your nervous system." "When I know what I'm fighting for, I don't waste energy on battles that don't matter."

I didn't have language for what I was carrying, so I carried it all. Every expectation. Every fight. Every performance of "I'm fine."

"We don't do that anymore" and "What am I fighting for?" started as survival tools. They showed up in the middle of spirals, self-betrayal, overstimulation, and moments I was about to give in or give too much.

I didn't realize it at the time, but those two questions started changing my nervous system. They gave me pause when I was spiraling and power when I felt helpless.

Now: These two phrases are my compass now. Not just words, but "We don't do that anymore" is the boundary I set with old patterns, especially self-doubt, people-pleasing, perfection, and over-functioning.

"What am I fighting for?" pulls me out of the fog and back into alignment. It reminds me I don't have to carry everything. I just have to choose what actually matters.

It's not about being strong every moment. It's about being intentional with your energy...and brave enough to walk away from anything that's not worth it.

What Helped:
-Sticky notes with reminders
-Saying "We don't do that anymore" *out loud*, even when it felt silly
-Filtering decisions through alignment instead of approval
-Tapping, breathwork, and nervous system resets when my body felt louder than my brain

To You, If You're Still Battling Everything: You don't need to win every fight. You don't need to earn your rest or prove your worth by powering through. Sometimes, the most radical thing you can do is pause, say, "We don't do that anymore," and walk away from the war you've been waging against yourself. That's not weakness. That's wisdom.

And if you're still caught in the fog? Ask yourself gently:

"What am I fighting for?"

Even if no clear answer comes, the asking is powerful. It gives your breath somewhere to land. You're still in it. And that means something. Let that be enough for now.

Chapter 12:

Don't Put Money on a Pedestal

Then: Money was a shapeshifter. A mirror I didn't ask for, reflecting back all the ways I felt not enough. I didn't just want it...I needed it. For proof. For safety. For a sense of worth. I let money drive my decisions, even when they weren't aligned. I priced low out of fear. I overbooked myself to feel secure. I shaped my life around earning, and called it success...even when it didn't feel good.

Now: I still care about money. I still want overflow. But I no longer let it boss me around.

I've made decisions that didn't make sense on paper but felt right in my soul and I've never regretted the ones led by alignment.

We're not "rolling in it" right now. Honestly, we're in a low season again. But it's different now. We're not suffering our success. We're living our values and trusting the money to rise up and support that.

I don't want my joy on pause until the numbers look right. I want the life I'm building to be the proof.

What Helped:
-Repeating: "I let values drive my decisions, not money."
-Choosing assurance over desperation.

-Letting celebration coexist with struggle.
-Shifting affirmations from performance to re-direction.
-Rehearsing peace, even before it made sense on paper.
-Asking, "Are we suffering our success?" as a gut-check.

To You, If You're Still in Scarcity: You are not irresponsible for wanting a life richer in more than just dollars. You are not behind. You are not a failure because the math isn't mathing right now.

But don't let money gaslight you into self-betrayal. Don't wait for overflow to believe in your own enoughness. You get to lead with your values now. You get to speak to the Universe with your choices. And every time you do, money stops being the master...and starts becoming the mirror.

It believes you. So, tell it the truth you want echoed. Say it with your breath. Your boundaries. Your bank account.

You don't need to perform for it. You just need to stay in alignment long enough to receive what's already on its way.

Chapter 4:

Does This Bring Me Energy or Take My Energy?

Then: I didn't know how to name it, but I was tired in a way rest couldn't fix. Not exhausted...just dulled. Like my soul was on low battery, and I couldn't find the charger.

I kept saying yes to things because I thought that's what strong women did. I didn't realize I was over-giving to stay safe. Overextending to stay relevant. Showing up when I was running on fumes and calling it strength.

And honestly? I wasn't even sad. I was just... disconnected.

Now: I say no without apology. I say yes with intention. I let my body tell the truth before my brain tries to rationalize over it.

"Does this bring me energy or take my energy?" is a question I now live by.

I no longer treat rest like a reward...I treat it like a responsibility.

And the wildest part? People respect my boundaries more when I actually honor them. Including me. Because when you stop abandoning yourself to make others comfortable, something beautiful happens: you become a safe place for you.

What Helped:
-Energy inventory (daily, weekly, whenever I feel "off")
-Saying no without a follow-up paragraph
-Letting "joyful participation" be the filter...not obligation
-Recognizing over giving as a form of hiding
-Remembering that not everything that drains you is bad...but it does need boundaries

To You, If You're Overextending: You're not selfish for wanting sustainability. Boundaries aren't barriers...they're bridges to a life that loves you back. You don't need to earn your worth by burning yourself out. Let your energy be your compass, your lifeforce, and your filter. Build a life around what actually gives you energy and watch how it blossoms. Just lean in to what feels *true* for you!

Chapter 17:

Grey Days & Alignment

Then: There wasn't always a reason. No breakdown. No loud, clear cry for help. Just a heaviness, that familiar numbness, and a floating sensation where I wasn't fully in my body but kept pretending to function.

Obviously now you know I call them grey days. But back then, I didn't honor them.

I blamed myself for them. I tried to perform through them. I kept pushing...thinking if I just got enough done, the fog would lift.

But it never did.

Because what I actually needed was permission to stop performing wellness and start practicing self-honesty.

Now: I still have grey days, but I meet them differently now. I soften. I name them. I say out loud, "This is a grey day," and in doing that, I stop the spiral.

I don't treat stillness like failure anymore...I treat it like information. When the fog comes in, I don't bulldoze through. I don't chase joy I can't catch. I let the quiet speak. And sometimes, it tells me everything I didn't know I needed to hear. Because grey isn't the problem. Avoiding it is. Trying to fill it with "over productivity" is.

What Helped:
-Naming the day before judging it
-Canceling obligations without apology
-Listening to my nervous system before my to-do list
-Making soft clothing and warm drinks part of the plan, not the exception
-Saying "no" and letting the silence be sacred
-Looking for alignment, not adrenaline
-Recognizing when my soul was asking for rest, not results

To You, If You're in the Grey: It's okay. First and foremost. It's okay.
You are allowed to feel off and not explain it. You're allowed to cancel. You're allowed to re-align. You're allowed to slow down. Take the nap. Wear the hoodie. Watch your favorite show.

Let your home, your schedule, and your friendships realign around who you're becoming...not who you've been *pretending* to be.

Chapter 14:

Laugh, Play Music, Make a Soundtrack to Your Life

Then: Everything felt flat. I wasn't sad, I was just... numb. I'd forgotten how to feel joy on purpose...not just when it stumbled in by accident. Music had disappeared from our daily rhythm, and with it, so did my spark. I was surviving my life with the volume turned down. And I didn't even notice... until I did.

Now: Music is the medicine now. Play is sacred. I laugh louder. I sing off-key. I dance while doing dishes and let my kids witness joy in real-time...not just in the highlight reel. Our life has a soundtrack again. Not because everything is perfect, but because we've chosen to press play anyway. Joy isn't waiting on the other side of healing. It's woven into it. And now, even in the chaos, I look for the songs that hold me.

What Helped:
-Silly playlists
-Blasting old emo tracks with my kids and letting the nostalgia connect us
-Letting music guide the mood instead of forcing one
-Laughing mid-spiral
-Giving myself permission to feel good without having to earn it

To You, If You Feel Numb: Joy isn't a luxury. It's a lifeline. Even if it's just one ridiculous song while folding laundry, let yourself have it. You don't have to wait until you feel better to dance. You don't have to deserve fun. You are allowed to feel it.

Start small. One song that you just *feel deeply*. Make a playlist for the season of life you're in – even if it's survival. Let the music hold you. Turn it up.

Chapter 19:

The Phone Isn't the Problem—Your Phone Diet Is

Then: I thought my phone was the problem. The constant distraction. The mental spiral. The disconnection. But it wasn't the phone. It was what I was feeding myself every time I opened it. Comparison disguised as inspiration. Self-help disguised as shame. Escapism dressed up as connection. I didn't need to quit my phone...I needed to reclaim how I was using it.

Now: I still scroll sometimes. I still get caught up sometimes, but now I catch myself. I pause. I notice. I ask: "What am I actually reaching for?" I take walks instead of diving into rabbit holes. I've made my phone quieter, simpler, less of a siren. I use it as a tool, not a trap. Not because I'm perfect, but because I'm trying to stay present.

What Helped:
-Turning off non-essential notifications

-Clearing my home screen completely
-Creating rituals instead of falling into reflexes
-Unfollowing accounts that spoke to my shame, not my soul
-Letting the scroll reflect my healing...not my hiding
-Naming the moments when I wanted to check out...and choosing to check in instead

To You, If You Feel Drained: You don't have to quit your phone. Just get curious. What are you actually reaching for? Start there. Start by paying attention to what you consume and how it makes you feel. Not everything that's popular is good for your nervous system. Not everything that's helpful is helpful *for you*. You are allowed to be unavailable. Your peace is worth protecting.

Chapter 20:

For Real, Not For Show

Then: I was so good at looking okay, I almost believed it myself. I knew how to post just enough to seem brave without being seen. I crafted captions like armor. I filtered my breakdowns into digestible poetry. I confused visibility with vulnerability. I thought being "real" meant being relatable. But deep down, I was still protecting the parts of me that actually needed the love.

Now: I don't need my healing to be inspirational. I just need it to be honest. My biggest shifts happen in silence, behind the scenes, off the screen, away from the noise. Not everything has to be shared to be sacred. Now, when I feel the urge to perform my progress, I ask: Is this truth or performance? And if it's performance, I pause. I soften. I come back to me. Because I don't need to be witnessed to be real.

What Helped:
-Letting my truth matter, even when no one claps
-Taking breaks from posting to be present
-Holding sacred moments privately, just for me
-Saying no without performing softness
-Choosing embodiment over explanation
-Reminding myself that I don't need to prove my healing to live it

To You, If You're Still Performing Progress: You don't owe anyone a curated version of healing. The real kind is messy. You're allowed to heal in silence. You're allowed to post...or not post. Just do what feels right...to you. It's just about knowing what your intentions are. Don't feel the need to perform.

Chapter 24:
The Day I Almost Quit

Then: I was mid-way through writing this book and drowning in doubt. I wasn't sure if my words mattered, if the healing would stick, or if any of it was ever going to add up to something useful. It wasn't loud or dramatic...it was the kind of quitting that happens in silence. The kind where you stare at the ceiling and wonder if maybe invisibility is safer after all.

Now: I'm still here. Still showing up. And I can say, with full breath in my chest, the Universe wasn't punishing me...it was preparing me. That season wasn't a dead end. It was a recalibration. A pause to make sure I didn't just write this book, I lived it. Now, when I feel the heaviness creep back in, I remember breakdowns don't cancel the dream. They clarify it.

What Helped: Letting one tiny thing matter each day. Trusting the nudge even when I couldn't see where it led. Saying out loud, "The Universe *is for* me," until I started to believe it. Letting the page hold what I couldn't. Walking away for a minute without walking away forever.

To You, If You Feel Like Giving Up: Don't confuse the quiet with failure. Don't confuse the fog with a lack of progress. The middle is messy for everyone. But you are not late. You are not lost. You're in the part of the story where the character almost turns back...and doesn't. Keep going. You don't have to believe in yourself every second. Just long enough to take the next step.

A Word About Self-Help Books (Including This One)

I love self-help books. But here's what I wish someone told me: the more you consume, the more paralyzed you can become. Not because the tools don't work, but because you become so *aware* of everything you could do that you end up doing... nothing.

If that's you, let me say it plain: You don't need more books. You need more moments.

Pick one tool. Use it today. Not perfectly. Just use it. Let integration be messy. Let it be yours. Don't put this book on a pedestal. Scribble in the margins. Rip pages. Revisit the ones that echo. Ignore the ones that don't.

This wasn't written to be believed. It was written to be lived.

You Don't Have to Arrive. Just Keep Returning.

This isn't the end. It's a checkpoint. A breath. A pause to acknowledge that healing doesn't always roar. It often whispers.

Whatever part of your story you're in... you're not alone in it.

I'm still becoming. Still choosing. Still listening. Still believing. And if nothing else, I hope you remember this:

Your growth is not behind schedule. Your becoming is right on time.

CHAPTER TWENTY-EIGHT

LET HER DIE (AGAIN AND AGAIN)

Y ou think you've healed? Write a book about it. Seriously. If you want to meet every version of your doubt, your fear, your ego on full display, try putting your truth in print. Try telling the world you're ready to be seen. Try showing up without a filter and saying, *"This is me, this is real, and I believe it matters."*

She'll come for you. Every damn time. Even now, **here**, at the end, I find myself still fighting the same fight. I almost scrapped the book. Started chipping away at it. Editing it to death. Smoothing it down until it didn't sound like me anymore. I didn't even realize I was falling into the same old pattern. Second-guessing. Letting Ego have her time in the sun, yet again. I heard her voice on repeat:

"Fix it."
"Make it better."
"You're not quite enough."

I spent four hours last night shrinking it down. Diluting it. Quieting myself. Because deep down, I didn't believe this voice was worthy of being heard.

But that's the pattern, right? That's the part we don't talk about enough. Even after all the wins. Even after all the healing. There's still that whisper. That subtle pull back into smallness.

It sounds like logic. It feels like humility. But it's ego in disguise.

And the worst part? She doesn't show up when you're failing. She shows up when you're leveling up. The moment you claim space...The moment you dare to be heard...She slinks in, dressed like doubt, and says, *"You sure this is yours to say?"*

I've felt it in the quiet. But I've also felt it in the spotlight.

A podium. I'm just up there, talking about my experience. And then it creeps in—that voice. That background worry whispering, *You're too much.* You're making yourself seem too bold, too sure, too something...

Not "you're not enough" this time...now it's the opposite: *You're too loud. Too honest. Too exposed.*

That's how ego plays both sides. She tells you you're too small to matter... Then tells you you're too much to be loved. And there she is again, creeping in like she always does. Not with facts. With fear. Even when I think I've silenced her, she finds another way in.

You don't kill her once. You have to keep killing her. Over and over.

It's not a one-time burial. It's a practice. A vigilance. A daily discipline.

Because every new space you enter? She's waiting there. Every unfamiliar room. Every next-level opportunity. She rises up and says, *This is scary. This is uncharted. This is not for you.* She tugs the leash and pulls you back toward safety.

Even if you've climbed a dozen mountains, the next one will still trigger that same damn fear. That same resistance. That same script. So, what do you do?

You slay the dragon again.

And again.

And again.

That's what the healing journey is. Not one mountaintop, but a whole mountain range. Not one breakthrough, but many. And each one will require a deeper version of you. A braver version.

There is no finish line. No pot of gold. No "healed to perfection."

But there *is* progress. There *is* awareness. There *is* strength.

And most of all…there's choice.

To let your ambition be louder than your fear. To let your dreams outshout your doubt. To choose bravery over comfort, even when your ego begs you not to.

Deciding to be brave is not a one-time decision. It's a spiral. A rhythm. A muscle.

Some people won't even do it once. But if you can do it once, you can do it twice. And if you can do it twice, you can do it for the rest of your life.

So, let's get one thing straight: This is not the part where you close the book and become someone new forever.

This is the part where you realize: **this isn't the end.**

This is the practice.

You don't read a book like this to fix one thing and walk away. You read it to remember. This is how we return to ourselves. This is how we rise.

That version of you (the one who needed to stay small, who wanted to hide, who performed instead of lived) she doesn't go quietly. She doesn't die once. She shows up every time the terrain changes. Every time the frontier expands. Every time you dare to reach for more.

You'll think you've slain the dragon... and then a new one shows up in a different disguise. And you'll question yourself again. You'll wonder if you're really cut out for the life you say you want.

And you are. But only if you keep choosing to be.

You don't just *become* the new version of you and then coast. I wish it were that easy. But it's not. Instead, you choose her, daily. You return to her when you forget. And you will forget. Or you'll get caught up in life. But either way, you'll find your way back. I promise.

You'll recommit when you slip. You'll remember when the fog rolls in. And it'll sound like this quiet whisper: *"The tools carried me before. I can find them again."*

You don't get to build her just to survive a hard season. You build her to carry you forward. To be your standard now. To become your default.

And it's okay if you forget. Or if you fall off. But sweetheart, just come back. Come back as many times as you need. That's what a practice is. That's what a spiral is.

This is the work.

And this, this right here, is where your life begins again.

Before You Go
This wasn't just another self-help book. It was a mirror. A map. A subtle nudge and a sharp push, depending on what you needed. And if you're still here, if you made it through the grey days, the money chapters, the mindset shifts, the garage sessions, the vulnerable moments, let me say this loud and clear:

I'm proud of you. You're on the path. You're not hiding anymore. Not fully. Not like before.

Sure, there will still be days when you feel yourself slipping. Days when the covers feel safer than clarity. When you shrink to fit someone else's version of "enough." When you consider abandoning your voice to keep the peace.

But the difference now?

You'll catch it. You'll notice the tension in your chest when something's off. You'll feel that inner tug-of-war between your ego and your soul. You'll pause before you spiral. You'll speak up when it counts. You'll hold space for others...*without* disappearing in the process.

Success doesn't require the sacrifice of self. Visibility doesn't require perfection. And love (real love) can hold all of you, not just the curated parts.

Maybe you cracked yourself open in these pages like I did. Maybe you revisited old wounds. Maybe you just read with curiosity and aren't ready to dive all the way in yet. That's okay.

I hope somewhere in here, you laughed at an old thought spiral because you finally saw it for what it was. I hope you sat with your shadows and danced with your light. I hope you stopped seeing yourself as broken and started seeing yourself as *becoming.* You've taken inventory... of energy, of joy, of misalignment, and of control. You've faced your tendency to carry everything alone. And now? Now you know:

You're allowed to let it be easier. You're allowed to want different things than you used to. You're allowed to pivot. You're allowed to say no. You're allowed to take breaks. You're allowed to take up space. You're allowed to trust yourself, even when others don't get it yet. You've built your toolkit. Now you get to live it. Not for approval. Not for perfection. But for you.

A LETTER FROM THE AUTHOR

If you made it here, thank you. Truly. Not just for reading, but for staying. For showing up with your whole heart and letting mine speak to yours. Writing this book cracked me open in ways I didn't expect. There were chapters I didn't want to write. Moments I didn't want to admit. Truths I didn't know how to say until they were already on the page.

This book is a collection of the battles I've fought...out loud, in silence, in front of mirrors, and in the middle of beautiful, messy chaos. And maybe you saw yourself in some of those pages. Maybe you met your own voice between the lines.

If so, I hope you felt less alone. I hope you felt seen. I hope you remembered what you're capable of. Because the truth is, I didn't write this book to tell you who to be. I wrote it to remind you that you already are. She's in there (buried maybe, bruised maybe) but still breathing.

And if this book handed you a shovel, a sword, or a light switch... then it's done its job. Please don't treat this as a finish line. You can return to these words any time. Let them echo when it's dark. Let them challenge you when you're slipping. Let them hold you when you forget who you are.

This isn't just a book. It's a conversation. And I'm still listening.

Much Love, XO
Melissa Dean

ACKNOWLEDGEMENTS

This book didn't come from one version of me—it came from all of them. The lost ones. The loud ones. The quiet ones who still showed up. And the people who held space for every single version of me.

Koko— You have been my anchor, my calm, my chaos translator, and the steady voice when my own went quiet. Thank you for holding the weight with me, for believing in me when I doubted myself, and for listening to all the versions of this book before the world ever saw a word of it. You have always seen the bigger picture, even when I could only see the mess. This book wouldn't exist without you. Neither would the version of me who finally finished it. Thank you for helping me process the grey days. For helping me untangle my thoughts and ideas and having conversations every night about it. For allowing me to obsess over my projects. For always, always holding space. You are my best friend. My everything. I am so proud of the healing journey you've been on. You are showing up and you are such a great role model. I love you more than you'll ever know.

To my three wild, soulful kids— May you always trust your knowing and never feel like you have to hide your light to keep others comfortable. Watching you grow reminds me what this is all for.

Mason, my mirror— I see so much of myself in you. You've challenged me in ways that forced me to grow. You reflect back to me the parts I've avoided and the strength I didn't know I had. You remind me to think deeply, speak honestly, and stay true to who I am, even when it's hard. You continue to teach me to show up for myself, even when the world has different expectations of you. As I help guide you through, you are also guiding me. Your hugs and chats are everything. We are both misunderstood. We are both pushing the limits. We are both not enough and so much more than what was expected of us. I am so grateful for you. I am so proud of you. I love you. The conversations in Jupiter and the turtles on the beach are my favorite recent memories. That one turtle that came out of the water RIGHT in front of us-no coincidence there.

Mia, my healer— Your softness holds more power than the world knows what to do with. You see the hearts of others so clearly. You've taught me that gentleness isn't weakness, and that true healing happens in the quiet moments no one else sees. You continue to teach me that competition can be met with love and you live that truth. You remind me, just by being you, that I am enough. Your hugs always seem to come at the exact moment I need them most. You are healing my inner child with every small act of love. You are fierce, passionate, and always rising, and in doing so, you inspire me to rise, too. You raise the bar not just for yourself, but for me as well. I am so grateful for you. I am so proud of you. I love you.

Micah, my patience— You are joy and fire and mystery wrapped into one. You've stretched my understanding of time, presence, and grace. You have handled every setback with a smile. You have exceeded every limitation that was placed on you and continue to do so. You teach me how to slow down, how to laugh when everything feels heavy, and how to stay curious, even when I'm tired. You are my teacher and have shown me that just because we see things one way, there are always other paths. Your hugs when you sense I'm having a hard day? They carry me through. I am so grateful for you. I am so proud of you. I love you.

My parents—thank you for cheering me on, even when you didn't always understand the path I was taking. Your constant support and willingness to shuttle kids from one place to another has been part of the foundation that built this.
-Mom, our daily morning chats, navigating the chaos, reframing the mess, and reminding me that every detour is just another adventure, have helped me keep moving forward. You have this way of listening and letting me ramble until I find the answer myself. You've been my sounding board, my mirror, and my compass. You've reminded me who I am on the days I forget. When I'm overwhelmed, when I'm doubting, when I'm spinning in circles...you help me

find the thread again. And more than anything, thank you for holding space for the version of me that was still becoming.

-Pops, thank you for always supporting, always answering my calls, and always, always helping bring my crazy ideas to life. You've taught me that you don't have to read the instructions to build something great—and that sometimes, trusting your gut and getting your hands dirty is the best way forward. Whether it was fixing a broken door, building a million different props, or problem-solving something you knew nothing about just because I needed it—you always show up. With quiet strength. With a solution. With a sense of calm that steadies me. You've shown me what it looks like to love through action. To believe in someone, even when their path doesn't make sense on paper. And to stand back, without trying to take over, while still being ready to jump in the moment I ask.

Mana—the only one outside of my husband and kids who knew I was writing this. Thank you for always being the one who listened without trying to fix. The one who held space without needing to be the loudest voice in the room. You've always known I was a little different than the rest of the family—and that quiet, unwavering understanding has carried me more times than I can count. In a world that often felt too loud, your presence reminded me it was okay to move slower, feel deeper, and do things my own way.

Stephie—You've always been a force. From the time I was little, you were my favorite. I watched you parent your boys with a kind of boldness and heart that stuck with me. You didn't sugarcoat things. You didn't back down. You said what you meant and meant what you said. Fierce, funny, and full of fire. You taught me that you don't have to take no for an answer if it doesn't sit right in your bones. That conversations with strangers can make the world feel smaller. That life is meant to be lived out loud. I still admire your ability to speak your truth without shrinking and I carry those lessons with me...even the ones I'm still learning how to live out. Thank you for being a walking permission slip to be bold, to be real, and to have a damn good time while doing it.

TaLeah—For being the constant. My sister in every way that counts. From six years old to now, you've been there, through every season, every shift, every storm. You've seen the awkward, the angry, the heartbroken, the growing versions of me, and you never left. Your presence in my life is one of the greatest gifts I've ever been given. I love you more than words can say. Thank you for being my safe place, my mirror, my memory-keeper, and my always.

Crystal—without you, I wouldn't be where I am today. You introduced me to the spiritual side of life. You ushered me to new ways of thinking, healing, and being. Your tough love pulled me back when I started slipping off my path. Your steady presence, whether it's in the form of a message, or just a knowing reminder, has always grounded me. I wouldn't be here today without you. You probably have more patience for me than anybody else. Thank you for seeing me before I knew how to see myself.

Chels—For being the guide. For showing up with sage and presence when I didn't have the words. For sitting with me in my unraveling without ever needing me to tie it up in a bow. You've always held space for both the mess and the magic. You've spun me into my deepest depths, not to abandon me there...but to walk beside me until I surfaced again. You've reminded me, again and again, that the burden isn't mine to carry alone. That I'm allowed to fall apart without losing myself. That healing doesn't always look like light, it sometimes looks like letting someone else hold the torch when I can't. You are never more than a message away. Thank you for being the mirror, the medicine, and the reminder that I don't have to navigate this path alone. Thank you for being the spark that made this all take off.

Em—You've been one of my closest friends for as long as I can remember. Technically, I'm older, but I've always looked up to you. Your heart, your creativity, your constant belief in me, even when I couldn't see it for myself. You've been there through so many versions of me and through it all, you've never wavered. You show up with loyalty, laughter, and the kind of grounded love that makes everything feel possible. Now, watching you step into your own magic as the HMUA for my boudoir business—it feels full circle. (It's our own version of Search & Rescue) You're not just behind the scenes making women feel beautiful (though you do that flawlessly), you're part of the soul of this work. Thank you for walking beside me, believing in the dream, and being the kind of friend every girl deserves to grow up with.

KC—Like an aunt, a mentor, and a cheerleader all in one. You've always had my back, always believed in me, and always showed up with love and loyalty. Thank you for being a steady voice of encouragement through every chapter. I'm so grateful for you.

Alyssa—Thank you for being such a cheerleader and my biggest fan, even when life got chaotic. For never making me feel guilty about the canceled coffee dates, the missed texts, or the long gaps between catch-ups. Your steady support has meant more than you know.

My soul sisters, you know who you are, thank you for walking this road with me and reminding me of my light on the days I couldn't find it.

My friends—thank you for holding space, forgiving the radio silence, cheering for my wins, and staying through the mess. To every client who sat in my studio and cracked their heart open, you gave me the language. You gave me the proof. You gave me the honor of witnessing your becoming, and in doing so, gave me the courage to keep moving through mine.

Diane—Thank you for being one of the first people to make me feel truly seen and valued. You are a special soul.

Karli—The biggest ray of sunshine. Thank you for always supporting me. The world is a brighter place with you in it.

Brandi & Katie—For all the HS memories and laughter that helped shape me into who I am today. I wouldn't be here without you.

Denise—Thank you for always offering a helping hand. Always.

The Universe—thank you for the whispers and the wake-ups. The grey days and the breakthroughs. The synchronicities, the signs, the redirections, and the second chances. You never stopped showing up for me, even when I questioned you.

And finally, to the crazy version of me who decided to write this book in the middle of absolute fucking chaos, you were so tired, and you did it anyway. You showed up for your healing. You showed up for your message. You kept going when it would've been easier to hide.

To everyone I named—and even those I didn't but who still shaped me—thank you. You are part of her death and my rising.

With my whole heart,
—M

ABOUT THE AUTHOR

Melissa Dean is a boudoir photographer, mother of three, and spiritual troublemaker who believes in burning the old stories to build something braver. She writes the way she lives—raw, honest, and heart-first. Her words aren't polished for performance; they're written in real time, through the mess and the magic.

When she's not in the studio capturing women reclaiming their power, she's probably in the garage, barefoot, covered in ash, writing the next one. Or she's at the fields with her kids. Her work lives at the intersection of healing, identity, and fire, because some versions of you have to die before the real you can rise.

Follow her journey and upcoming projects at
www.letherdie.com
Instagram:
@let.her.die.book
@melissadeanboudoir
@melissa.is.healing

www.letherdie.com/111

www.ingramcontent.com/pod-product-compliance
Lightning Source LLC
Chambersburg PA
CBHW031458120626
46545CB00005B/1667